*Special thanks to Donna Dozier who edited this material and added many needed improvements.*

Cover Design:  Skip Moen and Donna Dozier

# 31

*Days of Transformation*

By

Skip Moen
and
Laurita Hayes

# Table of Contents

## Preface

*This little book came about because of the requests of readers of my website blog. When I wrote the analysis of the thirty-one verses I intended to direct readers toward self-examination. I was delighted to discover Laurita's insights added to the blog each day. Then several readers asked if I would make my material available in book form so that it could easily be shared as a whole. When I considered this possibility, I immediately realized that Laurita's comments and personal vulnerability greatly enhanced the exploration of the text, so I asked her to allow me to use her work as well. The result has been a wonderful combination that I hope will take each of you, not only deeply into the Bible, but also show you just how powerful personal involvement can be.*

*Be exceedingly blessed.*


*Skip Moen, Montverde, Florida*

*Laurita Hayes, Arnoldsville, Georgia*

**1.** *"Repent, for the kingdom of heaven is at hand."*
Matthew 3:2 NASB

## *Repent*

"He, who truly repents, is chiefly sorry for his *sins*. He, whose repentance is spurious, is chiefly concerned for their *consequences*. The former chiefly regrets that he has *done* evil; the latter that he has *incurred* evil. One sorely laments that he deserves punishment; the other that he must suffer punishment. One approves of the Law that condemns him; the other thinks he is harshly treated, and that the Law is rigorous. To the sincere penitent, sin appears exceeding sinful; to him who sorrows after a worldly sort, sin, in some form, appears pleasant. He regrets that it is forbidden. One says it is an evil and bitter thing to sin against God, even if no punishment followed; the other sees little evil in transgression if there were no painful consequences sure to follow."[1]

Plumer's comment about the appearance of sin as pleasant but forbidden is very instructive. The truth of the matter is that for some of us, sin does seem appealing. We just wish it weren't. We wish we had a vile hatred for sin so that it would be easier not to be tempted. But if we examine our actions very carefully, we just might find that the reason we try not to sin is that we fear the *consequences*. And

---

[1] Dr. William S. Plumer, *Repentance and Conversion*

if those consequences were removed, we might just go ahead with the anticipated act. <u>Until sin becomes putrid, it will always appeal.</u> Until we truly repent, we will be deterred but not altered.

Now Feinstein's insight that biblical pollution is firmly set within a cultural acquisition of what is disgusting makes perfect sense. The Torah isn't a set of rules that prevent us from doing what we really wish. The Torah is a way of teaching us about repulsion. The Torah creates a culture where some things are so repugnant, so vile, so offensive, that we just can't even *imagine* doing them. For the culture of Torah, sin is like drinking sour milk. It reeks to high heaven. Now we can appreciate Oswald Chambers' comment that for the true believer, there is no such thing as a "moral vacation." Saturnalia is a completely pagan holiday.

Now we also realize that John the Baptist did *not* use the Greek word *metanoeo*. This verb is derived from *noeo*, meaning "to perceive, to think, to know." It is about a *mental* state chiefly determined by cognitive processes. But sin isn't about *wrong thinking*. It is about *disgusting behavior*. "There can be no knowledge without emotion. We may be aware of a truth, yet until we have felt its force, it is not ours. To the cognition of the brain must be added the experience of the soul."[2] Until sin *makes me sick*, it isn't biblical. Repentance is not about changing my mind. It is about changing my moral taste buds. It is about acquiring the taste of heaven in a mouth made from the earth.

---

[2] Arnold Bennett

8

So this is Day 1. Day 1 of what? Day 1 of learning to be disgusted by the tastes we have grown accustomed to. Day 1 of not simply deciding to practice righteousness but rather of *tasting* the vomit we have been consuming. Here's what I am proposing. Beginning today, and for the next 30 days, we will *eat* what we have sown so that we can reap what only God has planted. In other words, we will begin the process of truly hating sin, of finding it disgusting and nauseating so that we don't want anything to do with it. This will require some serious self-examination. We will have to dig deep into those hidden spots where only consequence really keeps us from moral vacations. We will have to endure some vomit, some purging, so that we can get rid of the toxic accumulation that we have come to view as normal. As Peter said, "As obedient children, do not be conformed to the former lusts *which were yours* in your ignorance," (1 Peter 1:14).

Write down that one thing that gnaws away at you, that one thing that you secretly wish just didn't have fearful consequences so you could get away with it. Write it down—and then *feel* the idea. What does it taste like? Is it in some way appealing? Time to throw up.

*Laurita writes:*

*I used to think repentance was something I manufactured to bring to the altar. Silly me. I cannot be repentant in my flesh because nothing in my flesh finds sin repugnant!*

9

*I then despaired of being able to repent sincerely, until I realized that the Word tells me that repentance is a GIFT! Oh! That means that I don't have to make it up, and it also means that I can ask for it! Now I go through my day asking to be sorry for (disgusted by) things that are not of G-d. Much better results! Does that then make it G-d's fault that I am not sorry? G-d forbid! It is MY responsibility to look into that perfect Law of liberty and see what I SHOULD be sorry for.*

*I have found something else. So often I have to be actually delivered from something BEFORE I find it repugnant. That makes sense, if you think about it. I naturally am in agreement with my own actions. That is the way I was made, in fact. It's not wrong, it's just human, but it means that in my flesh I cannot even find the correct way (reason) to repent! In my flesh all I can do is be sorry that it didn't work! I have to bring that disgusting(!) offering – my fake repentance – to the Temple like the polluted offering it is, and ask to have it redeemed – exchanged for a perfect one.*

*True repentance is like an alien force that crash-lands on my planet and splits my atoms apart. I was discussing the Second Law of Thermodynamics with my son, and he was observing that in a perfect world, atoms would not be decaying. Righteousness, I truly believe, resets even the physics of life; it superimposes a new reality – it rewinds our molecular clocks, so that our "youth is renewed like the eagle's". (So why am I going to die anyway? Perhaps it may be because some of the sins I have committed were "sins unto death" where, even though I am repentant and forgiven, have still sentenced me. But then, there were the perfected walks of Enoch and Elijah. I look at Moses, though, who repented but died.) So often I realize that I am being truly sorry (gifted with repentance) for something – repulsed and horrified by my actions – only AFTER I am delivered from it (from being in agreement with it). Deliverance, in fact, is a package deal. I get given not only the marvelous freedom from the bondage, but I also get given the correct reaction to it (disgust and just plain not interested anymore) after the fact, too. The miasma in front of my eyes and nose clears and I can see (and smell!) it for what it really is. And I used to think I had to do all that up front, in my own flesh, BEFORE I could get forgiven! No wonder I spun wheels for so long! Repentance in the flesh, then, is just another "dead works" – something that is going to get me dead. It is just another way to attempt to work my way to heaven.*

*I read somewhere that Yeshua is the only man who was able to repent perfectly, but that was because He had nothing to repent of. And He offers His repentance to me, as a gift. Then His baptism becomes mine. He warned me, though, to get ready to die (sure wouldn't want to be buried alive under that water!). Die to what? Sin. How? True repentance is a killer. It kills my flesh. And "no man yet hateth his flesh, but nourisheth it and cherisheth it". I cannot even kill myself correctly! So, every day, I ask Him to kill me. Softly. With His smile. He does. And though He slays me, yet I trust Him. Sure does beat getting myself killed by my own actions, though! Hallelujah!*

11

**2.** *As obedient children, do not be conformed to the former **lusts** which were yours in your ignorance,* 1 Peter 1:14

## Lusts

OK, so let's tone this down a bit. The Greek word is *epithymia*. Yes, it can mean "lust" but if we read it like this, we are likely to dismiss Peter's comment as not applying to us. After all, we aren't pedophiles or whoremongers or those other terrible sexual sinners. When we read the word "lust," we are inclined to think "sex." But we are proper, polite and (best of all) secretive. No one really knows what we actually desire (but are afraid to do). Who among us won't look if there's an opportunity to see what shouldn't be seen? Who among us won't consider what it would be like to take what shouldn't be taken? Who among us is still *transparent* as we were in the Garden. Naked and not ashamed. It isn't "lust" that is killing us. It's our emotional involvement with *desire*. It might be sexual desire, but it doesn't have to be. It could be the secret desire for power, for control, for fame, for fortune, for acceptance, for honor, for glory, for recognition or anything else that directs and shapes our behavior. You see, *epithymia* is simply the energy of the *yetzer ha'ra* given unrestrained expression. It's the emotional surge associated with having the world the way I want it.

Now you tell me: Is there anything in your life that seeks its own desire? Is there something you find about yourself that constantly wishes to take control? Have you discovered that under that veneer of careful respectability there is a monster that wants? What it wants doesn't really matter. That it wants, and won't be satisfied until it gets whatever it wants, that's what matters. Paul expressed it like this:

"For I know that nothing good dwells in me, that is, in my flesh; for the willing is present in me, but the doing of the good *is* not. For the good that I want, I do not do, but I practice the very evil that I do not want. But if I am doing the very thing I do not want, I am no longer the one doing it, but sin which dwells in me" (Romans 7:18-20).

*Epithymia* is an alien residing in my very being.

Peter notes that this alien force was on quite familiar terms in the past. Unless you lived in a Pollyanna world, you know exactly what Peter is talking about. In the past, all that *epithymia* energy drove you to act in your own self-interest. In fact, all that energy is what made you who you were. Perhaps we were all borderline pathological narcissists. The reason Peter exhorts us to be obedient children is because he knows (and so do we) how easy it is to revert to those former ways. We spent a lot of time in training camp learning those ways of self-fulfillment and self-protection. We fed the monster—often. Those ways became habitual, and it takes a long time to change a habit. Just ask the children of Israel wandering in the wilderness.

We have a serious task before us. Unfortunately, practice doesn't make perfect here. Practicing those old ways makes death. But, as perhaps you have already discovered, *stopping* isn't the answer either. Nature abhors a vacuum no less in emotional constitution than in astrophysics. Stop we must, but the hole left from abandoning the former practice of *epithymia* demands compensation. Even apathy is an emotion. It's just not a *sustainable* emotion. If we are going to refuse conformity with our former comforts, we will have to have a powerful substitute, but not another sedative. It is useless to try to live according to the Law without enlisting the power of a domesticated *yetzer ha'ra*. Such an attempt takes us right back to Romans 7.

What then, oh children of the dark? Where do we find such a remedy? From our Greek perspective, there is no hope here. There is no internal power of the self that can rescue us from those ingrained substitutes for *shalom*. Paul is right. We know what we want to do. We just can't do it. Good intentions make no real difference. But from a Hebrew perspective, there is an answer. It is not a gentle one, but it is perhaps the only one. The answer is, as Brené Brown so eloquently expressed, *vulnerability*! And that means *telling someone who you really are under the skin*. The answer is not simply confession to the invisible, all-knowing, benevolent God. That's half the solution (after all, He already knew). The answer is to let someone, some physically present flesh and blood someone, hear your story, your real story, including all the *epithymia* struggles. The answer is to grasp with both hands that you are broken to the core *just like everyone else*. That your story isn't unique but it's yours and that until you share it, it will be the monster in the closet rattling the chain you put on the door.

The Hebrew answer is community. The Greek myth of individuality was destroyed when YHVH saw that it was not good for Adam to be alone. As long as you think the Garden is a place of private revelry, you are lost. YHVH's answer to *epithymia* is *'ezer kenegdo*—the one who is me outside of me, the one who "sees" me for who I am. Adam had YHVH. It wasn't enough. You and I must have the "other" in order to become human, to domesticate the *epithymia* of our shadow lives.

*Laurita writes:*

*Wow. Preach it, brother.*

*His strength is my weakness. In the flesh, I see that verse backwards. I read it as if my fractures (weak places) are what He 'needs' to be Almighty! LOL! I think it is because, in the flesh, I experienced my weak places (the places where I was sinning, and therefore was trying to hide) as the places others desired most to 'find out' so as to take advantage of me. Y'all, the world may operate as if sin (fracture in relationships) is fine, but just try to bobble the ball even a little, and they are crawling all over you in a flash! People magazine is a cruel place to find yourself. In the flesh, I see vulnerability as being asked to voluntarily EXPOSE myself (as in FLASH – LOL!) to others; to set myself up to their ridicule of my shame; to hand over the crates of rotten eggs and tomatoes and pies to throw at me. In the flesh, righteousness (the vulnerability of connection)*

16

*looks like I am being asked, basically, to sit there and get myself snowed. I mean, going around flashing myself might not be so bad if I knew I had a (flesh) body that was a 10; but, then, who does? This is why the way of the Cross (vulnerability) is foolishness to those who are operating outside the Law (they know they aren't a 10!), but it is also a stumbling block to those who are trying to get that perfect set of rock-hard abs (total connection) before they go ripping open their raincoats, as per the exercise instruction Manual that their ancestors got personally handed on a mountaintop. (Hey; at this point, we're all screwed!)*

*In my flesh, I desire most to have all the accouterments of love: all the glory, all the fame, all the advantages that connections provide, in fact, but I desire them without those connections. I desire them without having to actually go through the ACTIONS of relationship; chief among them the action of making myself vulnerable – of baring my outlet to your plug. In the eyes of the flesh, in fact, vulnerability looks like self-professed shame. Now, mutual shame is the dirty little secret that makes all those who walk in their flesh brothers, yes, but they are actually more like partners in crime (and we all know there is no honor among thieves). At best, we see each other as drinking buddies: someone to commiserate, to hide, WITH. As long as nobody switches on a light we're all good without our raincoats, right?*

*To walk in righteousness, though, is to walk without shame, because righteousness is the place of honor. Shame, of course, is about fractured connections (unrighteousness). However, nobody in their flesh can walk through the front door of honor to get to that righteousness for the simple reason that they have to crawl through the hall of humility before they reach honor – as the Word tells us – but the closest the flesh is ever going to get to humility is SHAME. The bad news is, there is no way that shame can make me good. Shame can never give me the power I need to do right. I mean, it cannot even get me to a place of true repentance because repentance is about exposure, but all shame wants to do is hide. At the end of my day, shame is just another gauge on my dashboard. This is why the world is lost, in fact. I think it is because true humility comes from a place of freedom, but shame comes from a place of bondage. They have different fathers. Shame is a side effect of fracture, which is the side effect of a lie, but humility is a side effect of an encounter with a Person known as Truth.*

*Folks, I have some Good News (Gospel) to share. In fact, for me, this was the key to understanding vulnerability. Vulnerability is not shame. I will repeat myself. I do not think we are being asked to go through shame in order to connect with those around us. Vulnerability does not ask me to shame myself in order to have others accept me. That would be that tailgate party with the world, which asks that you show the shame card to prove you are a member of the Sin Club. The Torah Club, however, is asking no such thing. The Torah Club is asking that you go through a mountaintop experience (exposure) first, yes, but Torah points us the Way to that Mountain (is, in fact the only way to even find that Mountain); however, when we get there, the Mountain (Torah; or, Rules of Engagement) is what gives us an encounter with a Person, and His Name*

18

*is Truth. The entrance into this club takes the humility that is acquired when I come face to face with the Truth.*

*What is the truth? The truth is that it is all about Him. Shame is what I experience when I am looking at myself. Humility is what I am experiencing when I am looking at Him. Vulnerability is simply humility in the face of the truth – in the face of love. No shame necessary. The good news is that I confess my sins to Him first (repentance) before I confess them to others (vulnerability). Shame, in fact, to me, anyway, is the recognition that I am disconnected, but the only thing I can do with shame in my flesh is to cave in to the temptation (sin) to repent to the world, so as to bypass repentance to Him. I think this is the closest the world can come in its desperate need to achieve righteousness on its own terms. How many times did I attempt to confess my sin through shame, to others (if they caught me!), as well as to myself (I used shame as the fuel in my tank for a long time in an attempt to earn love). It doesn't work! However, when I give Him my weakness (sin), He can then give me His strength (righteousness; or, connection), and my shame (fracture) is healed. My shame (need) is safe only with Him, because only He has the remedy for it. I do not ever have to be ashamed of the gospel of Christ. And what is that gospel? That I have been offered deliverance from this body of shame! LOL! Shame is exposure before deliverance (weakness). Humility is exposure AFTER a Deliverer (power). Hallelujah! That is a mountaintop exposure that I can always afford! As long as my life is all about Him (my part), and He is perfect (His part), we're*

19

*good to go! His buddies then become my buddies,*
*and, y'all, He's got ALL the right connections!*

**3.** *Also some of the Asiarchs who were friends of his sent to him and repeatedly urged him* **not to venture** *into the theater.* Acts 19:31 NASB

## Sacred Moos

I don't worry too much about sacred cows. Cows are really pretty docile animals. They usually just go wherever they are led. I worry about what cows do. They moo. They make noise. They leave cow pies behind. They disrupt the peacefulness of the quiet earth. It is the *actions* of sacred cows that cause me concern. If you have a sacred cow, no problem. Just let it munch in its own field, contentedly consuming God's green earth. But if you cause your sacred cow to start bellowing, creating disturbance and demanding attention, then I'll have something to say. "Why don't you keep that sacred cow under control? I mean, if you want a sacred cow in your backyard, hey, be my guest. But don't let your sacred cow start crying for the attention of all the rest of the creatures in the Kingdom. It's *your* sacred cow. Feed it if you wish. But don't expect me to take care of *your* cow's mooing."

I suspect that most of us have a few sacred cows occupying the spaces between our considered opinions and our feelings of Presence. We need those cows to remind us that life is oh-so-peaceful. Pastoral paradise on four hoofs. In truth, we probably use those cows to provide us with the milk of justification. That's kind of like spiritual pasteurization. We heat up our rationalizations in order to remove any microbes of doubt. Fully convinced that *our cows have the right kind of milk*, we expect total homogenization where everyone else's sacred cows finally fall into alignment with our *lead* cows. The goal is *agreement*. No cream rising to the top. Just nice plain *uniformity*.

The problem with uniformity is its contempt of difference. But difference is the fodder of community. If you and I agree about everything, there is hardly any point in talking, is there? I can have that sort of conversation any time I like. Just listen to me. When there is no difference, there is no need to speak. Perhaps that's one of the reasons why sermons seem so boring. I am told what I already know and what I know I will hear another fifty times this year. God loves me. I'm a sinner. I need forgiveness. Jesus is the way. So what? All those sacred moos don't make me examine my chronic malnutrition. I've had enough sacred moo milk to make me vomit. I need a little chaos in my life—a little barb of disturbance, a little thorn in the flesh, a little cognitive dissonance. I need something that doesn't come homogenized. In the end, what I really need is pain. I won't stop trying to feed myself of moo milk until I know the nausea it produces. Cream rises to the top, but only if you don't emulsify the fat. Cream can only exist in a world that allows difference.

Here's a serious exercise for those of us who can no longer digest sacred moo milk. *Feel the pain.* Stop anesthetizing. Stop pretending. Stop avoiding. Stop. *Feel* what hurts in your life. Weep. Shake. Shout. Clench your fist and throw invectives toward heaven. Get real for a change. "No, I'm not fine, thank you very much. And if you really care about me, you will listen to my pain." We are really Greek when it comes to this kind of reality. The Greeks reasoned that if something bad can happen to you, it can also happen to me. Therefore, I really don't want to know *anything* about the hurts in your life. It's just too scary.

Did you notice that even Paul's friends didn't want him to "venture" into the crowd? It's interesting that the word here is *dounai*, from the verb *didomi* which means "to give." Paul's friends didn't want him to be vulnerable. They wanted him to keep it for himself, not to give his message to a hostile crowd. Blend in. Don't be different. The translators gloss the word so we don't see that vulnerability is about *giving*.

Go watch Brené Brown again.

https://www.ted.com/talks/brene_brown_on_vulner ability?language=en

Are you willing to be vulnerable—even with yourself?


*Beth C. Mehaffey provided the following comment. Thanks Beth.*

*Amazing truth here: People do expect total homogenization, alignment with lead cows; if they do, the cream will never rise to the top. Peoples' gifts and talents will never be fully realized. People are afraid to disagree; I think we fear that our ideas will be discounted as we struggle to determine what truth really is. We may fear ridicule from our spiritual siblings in the assembly and/or the brutal abuse of certain lead cows who might thrash us to pieces for questioning them or for having a different opinion; we may fear we won't survive such a beating to rise again or that we'd emotionally lose the desire and ability to test everything. We are all unique in many ways –including the way our minds are wired to think because our creator made us that way; life would be boring otherwise. I long for the day that people would be open to hearing my opinions without me feeling like I have to preface everything I say with a disclaimer or apology of some kind. I want my opinions to matter or have value in an open forum. I want to feel my thoughts have worth even if I may be partially wrong; I also want to kindly be informed if there might be something I haven't considered. I want to be built up, not torn down. I want my worth to be reaffirmed when there is a difference of opinion. I want to be able to openly say "I love you" to someone because I love the way they consistently study and interpret the Scriptures or because of the way they act like Yeshua toward me; I want to be able to do this without begin accused of something unholy. I want people to say, "This is what we think about this Scripture passage; what do you think?" I also want to have a Greek or Hebrew scholar who is willing to be my friend and help me out when my level of knowledge of the languages are a bit inadequate or when I don't have access to better language resources that I can't afford. I don't want people to withdraw from me just because we don't believe exactly the same way on a particular topic. Our study goals are the same. We study the same Scriptures and yet we reach totally different*

25

*interpretations at times. I find that frustrating; still, I want to be loved and accepted despite our differences. It's a balancing act to wade through unexpected responses and to maintain relationships after a difference of opinion. I want the freedom and ability to discover the enormous number of patterns, details, majesty, and beautiful tapestry in/of the Word of God. I want to be able to say, "Hey, look at what I've found. Isn't that awesome?" At times, I want them to respond, "wow, you're right!" instead of "no, that's stupid!" When we disagree, we need to learn how to do it in a kind and loving way. I want to be vulnerable with others because you can't have relationships without it but sometimes it hurts like fire when things turn out poorly. Sometimes you just have to step back and figure out when or with whom is it safe to be vulnerable again. That's not always easy; it's risky.*

**4.** *and they, having become **callous**, have given themselves over to sensuality for the practice of every kind of impurity with greediness.* Ephesians 4:19 NASB

## Sensory Deprivation

Day 4. We're working on feelings. In particular, we're working on what it means to feel our sins. As good Greek citizens, we have command of the theology of sin. The theology of sin is an examination of the duty to obey an ethical standard set up by God Himself. In this cognitive examination, we learn that sin is essentially rule-breaking. Being good means keeping the rules. Being bad means breaking the rules. So theologians tend to define sin as "any failure to conform to the moral law of God in act, attitude, or nature."[3] Correct, but ineffective, especially for those of us who grew up believing that rules are *restrictions* on personal *freedom*! What this means is that our idea of sin is at war with our idea of liberty. We have failed to see sin as anything *beyond* the scope of our rule-oriented, moral "law" conceptions.

Let's take a different approach. Imagine your child, the one you love, does something that causes him or her injury and, at the same time, injures others. How do you *feel*? Do you address that child like the judge behind the bench? "Well, you know you broke the law. You know the consequences. It's

---

[3] Wayne Grudem, *Systematic Theology*, http://www.thegravelperspective.com/blog/2013/10/23/grude ms-systematic-theology-chapter-24-sin

your fault. You must pay for your mistake." Is that how you *feel*? I doubt it. I'm guessing that you feel *broken-hearted*. I'm guessing that you are weeping inside. I'm guessing you feel the pain of your child's action as if it were your own. You feel the remorse. You feel the distress. You feel the anxiety. Maybe you feel it even if your child doesn't. The very fact that this is your child who has created such a catastrophe is enough to cause emotional chaos *in you*. Forget the rules! They don't matter much now. What matters is the pain, the hurt, the agony of seeing the one you love failing, falling and in trouble. You ache. You experience sorrow. You cry over this child.

"When He approached Jerusalem, He saw the city and wept over it," (Luke 19:41).

Sin is whatever breaks God's heart.

Callousness is not caring about what breaks God's heart. The real mark of the sinner is that he is *beyond* feeling how God feels. The Greek *apalgeo* is derived from two words that mean to cease to feel pain or sorrow, to be taken *away* from grief. In first-century Hebrew thought, this is the equivalent of no longer feeling shame, of being dead to our own screams of abandonment.

Rather than hear the sounds of broken hearts, we muffle the cries with powerful sedatives like sex, money and power. We harden our hearts to our own terrors. In the end, sin is whatever prevents us from hearing the Messiah crying.

*Laurita writes:*

*When I decided to re-start my relationship with my Father, I was 'coming in from the cold'; from the outside, and as such, I had to go look long and hard from that position at all that entailed. I had to see it all from those eyes. A lot of things looked different from there. I remember the most shocking thing I found comfort in – it was, in fact, the deciding factor for me – and that was the fact that there was an unpardonable sin, and, no, it was NOT because I was afraid of committing it! That fear has no redeeming power whatsoever to it, by the way. No, it was because I was suffering, most of all, from abandonment. Abandonment was the viewpoint I was coming from; the lens I had to filter everything through. I mean, the whole world looked like that to me! And it was unbearable. It produced a righteous rage that I had no argument against. That rage, in fact, bound me for a long time. I could find no reason not to be angry. (Know what? I still can't.)*

*The fact of the unpardonable sin was the deciding factor for me that convinced me that G-d loved me because, looking at it from His viewpoint, if there were no such thing as an unpardonable sin, it would prove that He does not truly love us. So what is the unpardonable sin? What is sin? Sin is fracture of relationship; sin IS abandonment, in fact. None of us can endure abandonment. If we could, sin would not be sin for us; we would be happy 'on our own'. But relationship is the nature of love, as abandonment is the nature of sin. A lover cannot abide to be abandoned. Not even G-d. The unpardonable sin is not where He abandons us, as He promises that He never will; no, the*

30

*unpardonable sin is where we have abandoned Him,
and that is a sin no lover can forgive. It breaks His
heart, and it stays broken because there is no
relationship to fix it. I knew that rage. That was
when I realized He and I were on the same page,
and not in opposition to each other. I finally found
something to agree with Him on! It was that, more
than anything else, that convinced me that He truly
loved me; loved me enough to abandon Himself on
that cross for me, instead. I finally understood Him!
Hallelujah!*

**5.** *and they, having become callous, have given themselves over to sensuality for the practice of every kind of impurity with* **greediness**. Ephesians 4:19 NASB

## *The Tolerance Principle*

Day 5. More is never enough. How many millions does it take to make a millionaire satisfied? Just one more. How many lovers do I need to make sure I am constantly wanted? Just one more. How much power do I need to know I am completely in control? Just a little more. But more is never enough.

Gerald May writes, "Tolerance is the phenomenon of always wanting or needing more of the addictive behavior or the object of attachment in order to feel satisfied. What one has or does is never quite enough. . . The essential dynamic of tolerance, then, is that one becomes used to a certain amount of something, and this accustomedness removes the desired effect and leads to the need for more."[4]

Paul understood this dynamic. He doesn't use the word "tolerance." He uses the Greek *pleonexia*, the *covetousness* of addictive desire. The LXX uses the word for *unlawful* gain, but we should not think that it is limited to money. Unlawful gain is whatever we desire (covet) that extends beyond the borders of the Torah. Torah is life. *Pleonexia* is the attempt to gather *more than life*, and as it turns out, what is more than life is death. A derivative of the same

---

[4] Gerald G. May, *Addiction & Grace*, p. 26.

root is used to describe the idolater. This kind of greed is lethal.

So why do we want it? May continues.

> The longer an addiction continues, the more things will become associated with it and the more entrenched it will become. Some behaviors or chemicals that produce rapid, direct, and powerful effects may result in addiction after only one or two experiences. Others may require many repeated experiences before they become entrenched. But regardless of how an addiction begins, the longer it lasts the more powerful it becomes. Attachments are thus like spreading malignancies, steadily invading and incorporating their surroundings into themselves. To apply the words of Isaiah, addictions are like "greedy dogs, never satisfied," or as Habakkuk said, "Forever on the move, with an appetite as large as sheol, and as insatiable as death."[5]

A war you cannot win. But you can admit it and weep. You can admit you began taking comfort in substitutes for the Presence. You can feel the true agony of being outside the Garden. It's not about the rules, is it? It's about having to hide. "Who told you that you were naked?" *Pleonexia* told me. As soon as I realized that this was not enough, I knew I was naked. I have been seeking covering ever since, shedding skin with each new attempt. God help me.

---

[5] Ibid., p. 86.

*Laurita writes:*

*That has to be the most succinct description of addiction I have ever read! I am copying this one to give to others! May I? Thank you so much, Skip!*

*I have wondered often what it is in us that causes us to seek out addictive behavior, and why we do. I know it is the evil substitute for relationship, as all addictions release endorphins; those neurochemicals that cause us to FEEL like we are connected; part of something larger than ourselves, a feeling that we must have to feel secure. We are herd creatures, like sheep; we feel safest when we are pressed shoulder to shoulder in the very middle of a crowd. That way we won't be picked off like those poor unfortunates who have made the sad mistake of winging it alone. Addictions make me feel as though I am safely plugged in to the commonwealth when, actually, because I have put Self first, I am not.*

*So what is the righteous place that lets me know I am in the Safety Zone for real? The place that produces that feeling of connection that is the true Holy of Holies, where the Curtain rips and I am finally There, in that Presence? The place that every addiction seeks to reproduce? I think what we seek is glory. Glory is the right place for us to stay, in fact. The only thing wrong about it is when we seek it in the wrong places and in the wrong ways. Glory lets us know when we are in the Presence of the Shekinah, directly in front of the Mercy Seat, which covers (or, in our case, recovers us to) that Law of relationship. Glory lets us know that we have arrived. I think we want to feel glorious;*

34

*victorious; we want to swoon in acclamations and vindications and hear "well done". What we want, more desperately than anything else, is to LOSE OURSELVES (that unbearable weight we have fallen for carrying around when we signed on to the worship of Self), and Glory is where I am in the Presence of something that is Bigger Than Me.*

*Failing all that, of course, I at least want to not have to realize that I am not there yet! I do not like to feel the feeling of just me, stripped of all that is not me (yet); to feel the weightlessness of the Deep Space I have created around myself in response to the lie that I must worship mySelf and I am Not Safe if I expose myself to relationship with all that is Not Me. It is that feeling of disconnection; that glass bubble that I have built every time I did not invest in trust and vulnerability that keeps me 'safe' from hearing, seeing, tasting and touching or smelling for myself to see that others are Good. That leaves me without the satisfaction that my spiritual senses must have. Addictions are the narcotics that I get handed if I show up in the ER of the world with my screamingly painful nerve endings that are raw and exposed because they are not connected to the rest of my Body.*

*I want to feel the "weight and power; power growing under weight" (Wordsworth) of glory. I want to drop the intolerable weight of Me by feeling the even greater weight of the full import of being connected to the great I AM. In that Presence, and only in that Presence, does Self get squashed in this Sumo wrestling match I have set myself up for when I set out to sin. I want to lose at the Brook Jabbok; I want a Lover on top of me; I want to have my total*

35

*attention diverted from Me. No earthly addiction, in the end, can give me what only true glory can, but there is only one way that I can get myself into the glory of the Presence, and that is to check mySelf at the door, like the overcoat (or snakeskin!) that it is, because it is only Self that has ever been in the way of that Glory.*

**6.** *For I will be like a lion to Ephraim and like a young lion to the house of Judah. I, even I, will **tear to pieces** and go away, I will carry away, and there will be none to deliver.* Hosea 5:14 NASB

## The Betrayal of God

Did you ever think God didn't care? Did you think that your self-absorbed pursuit of substitutes for divine Presence escaped His notice? Did you think He was shamed? Or grieved? Or anguished over you? What loving parent would not experience the pain of rejection, the humiliation of abandonment?

And so the response.

"I will tear you to pieces and go away." When YHVH utters words like these, we should fall face first and plead for our lives. Heschel's insight into the divine response to unbridled desire is important. "In the domain of imagination the most powerful reality is love between man and woman. Man is even in love with an image of that love, but it is an image of a love spiced with temptation rather than a love phrased in service and depth-understanding; a love that happens rather than a love that continues; an image of tension rather than peace; . . ."[6]

The Bible makes it abundantly clear. Idolatry is adultery. And the groom responds. Sin is betrayal and the husband reacts. Divine jealousy is no laughing matter. What will the Lord of hosts do with those children who betray His trust and care?

---

[6] Abraham Heschel, *The Prophets*, p. 50.

38

Ah, the lion comes. But not because we have broken some rules. If that were the reason, YHVH would send a judge. The lion comes because we have fornicated with the enemy. We have smeared the name of the Holy One in the beds of those who detest Him. We sought to fill our needs with our own devices and we ended up chasing the numbing pleasure of momentary relief. We loved love and we sought to make it happen. The lion comes to devour the putrid mess we have made of this marriage.

This, by the way, is the turning point. Not that we did anything to foster its healing effect. In fact, we most likely responded to the lion's roar with terror and did all we could to delay his arrival. But listen to Heschel again.

"More excruciating than the experience of suffering is the agony of sensing no meaning in suffering, the inability to say, 'Thy rod and Thy staff, they comfort me.'"[7] If we are to be rescued from our malignant attachments, they must be *destroyed*. The lion must tear and shred and bloody the landscape. If we cannot fathom that the teeth of destruction are the pathway to peace, we will never be rescued from the prison of tolerance we have constructed around ourselves.

"The root of all evil is, according to Isaiah, man's false sense of sovereignty . . ."[8] Under the influence of our addictions, we believed we were gods. We thought we could find our own solutions

---

[7] Ibid., p. 147.
[8] Ibid., p. 165.

to the emotional devastation that lurks under the surface of our carefully orchestrated lives. We acted as if life belongs to us and should be experienced according to our designs. The lion comes from a different reality—a reality of divine determination.

A lion can crush the skull of an antelope with a single swipe of its paw. But it rarely does so. Instead, it toys with its prey, playing the death spiral, often eating while the victim is still alive but powerless. YHVH comes as the lion. Do not expect to die easily. Every tear of the flesh releases the accumulated toxins of self-satisfaction until there is no blood left to shed. Then God can give life—but not until then.

Today is the day you bleed.


*Laurita writes:*

*Meaninglessness is the basis of despair. There was no worse despair than that which I experienced when I thought that there was no purpose to my suffering; no redemptive quality to my pain. I needed the nobility of knowing that it MATTERED that I hurt – and it would have mattered if I knew someone CARED.*

*I didn't know that it was I that determined whether or not my suffering mattered! I had power over my suffering to the extent that I could make choices about it. In the seminal book Man's Search For Meaning, Victor Frankl writes about the two different classes of people that the suffering of the concentration camps produced: those to whom life had meaning, and those to whom it did not. One class produced survivors; the other produced victims. It was the exact same conditions for both: the question is, what was it that separated them? What I found in my little hell was that it was up to me to determine what my suffering meant. Oh, I tried all the obvious ways first. I denied it: that didn't work, it only made me depressed. I tried self-pity, hoping someone else would chime in: instead, others just hurried faster to get themselves to the other side of the road! I tried blaming others (hoping they would then feel enough guilt to take responsibility for my misery), but that made me schitzo. I tried blaming myself, but that gave me Chronic Fatigue, as the whips of Drivenness and Performance kept me in chronic adrenaline realities. I tried cutting deals with the devil, as he appeared to be the only one in the room with me, but I failed at being a badass; I mean, there were always hostages in my life: there were others who had no one but me; that I was being blackmailed with, in fact, and I had to play it straight for them. At the end of my day, I had found no way in my flesh to create meaning for my suffering, so, I blamed G-d. I thought that if it were His fault, then He would have to fix it! When He didn't, I felt that that 'proved' that He had abandoned me, and my rage just grew.*

*In Tolkien's Lord Of The Rings, Aragorn battles the chief of the Orcs, and, in the movie, as he finally runs him through with his sword, the Orc doesn't even slow down, but grabs that sword with his hands and pulls himself along it – totally intent on the purpose for which he was created – to get himself within reach of Aragorn (however, he dies before he makes it). That picture has simply been the best illustration for me of how I need to face obstacles that seemingly prevent me from fulfilling my purpose for which I was created. I have dubbed it "walking the sword", which is to say, use the momentum of disaster in your life: embrace the disaster as the opportunity it most certainly always is. All, all, is a gift from His hand. Start there. At some point beyond 'my' reasons and purposes, lie His. The correct choice of response to trouble at that point is Gimli the dwarf's response when he was asked if he thought they should fight to defend Helm's Deep: "Certainty of death, small chance of success – what are we waiting for?" If I do not understand that it all comes from His hand: both the 'evil' and the 'good' (and how would I know how to tell which is which?), then I am not going to be able to embrace everything in front of me equally with one single response: GRATITUDE! I am commanded to be thankful for everything. Until I learn exactly what that entails, I am not going to be able to be comforted by that Rod and that Staff.*

*The meaning of my suffering is that it shows me that it is NOT all about me! Suffering shakes me loose from my self-absorption, because at that point I can sincerely wish that it was NOT all about me! Only suffering can show me this. Success never will. The day I make a decision to start from a basis other than ME to determine meaning in my life is the day that that meaning has the room it needs to exist. I am not an island! The meaning in my life: its sufferings and successes, comes from it being about something BIGGER than me. Imagine that!*

**7.** *"Were they ashamed because of the abomination they had done? They certainly were not ashamed, and they did not know how to **blush**;"* Jeremiah 8:12 NASB

## Essential Embarrassment

Why don't we know how to blush? Actually, I'm afraid we do know the feeling. We just suppress it in order to pursue the *yetzer ha'ra*. But blush we must if God is going to turn us around. It doesn't take much practice. In fact, it takes no practice at all. Blushing is a natural emotional response associated with embarrassment, the experience of awkward self-consciousness in a moment of culturally conditioned shame. Someone who has no ability to blush is someone who does not share the same social fabric. From the perspective of the Bible, this is someone who has numbed himself to Torah conflict. It is the equivalent of offering your Jewish guests shrimp cocktail before dinner and then realizing what a fool you just made of yourself.

When Jeremiah employs the expression, he has something more in mind than social *faux pas*. "*kālam* denotes the sense of disgrace which attends public humiliation. In thirty cases the root is used in parallel with *bôš* 'to be ashamed' (q.v.). Any distinction between the meanings of the two roots is therefore small. However, when *kālam* appears by itself it does not often have the idea of disgrace which comes through a failed trust (a prominent element in *bôš*). Rather it is a more general disgrace resulting from any kind of humiliation. The fact that the Arabic cognate means 'to wound' suggests the idea of a 'wounded' pride."[9]

Do you know what else it suggests? A *wounded* God. When we no longer blush (*kalam*) from our transgressions, we wound God. He designed an automatic emotional early warning system in the cultural training of Torah. Blush is essential embarrassment. That little shot of adrenaline, that moment of blood rush to the surface of the face, that instantaneous pang of potential humiliation – these are designed to alert you to overstepping the cultural boundaries in a Torah observant society.

Of course, when you don't live in a Torah observant society your blush factor is reduced sometimes to insignificance. You *feel nothing*, and as a result, you continue in the behavior that will someday cause you enormous regret, shame and remorse. What can you do *now* in Babylon to hone the blush reaction? You can tune your consciousness to the feelings of YHVH. You can ask, "Would this wound God?" before you act. That might not be enough given the prior training you accepted as a student of Babylon, but it is a start. You can read the Bible for its emotional conditioning about the heart of God. You can ask Him to let you feel what He feels. And you can refuse to push aside the blush when it comes. It's there for your benefit. At last, a useful hot flash. Day 7.

---

[9] Oswalt, J. N. (1999). 987 כָּלַם. In R. L. Harris, G. L. Archer, Jr. & B. K. Waltke (Eds.), *Theological Wordbook of the Old Testament* (R. L. Harris, G. L. Archer, Jr. & B. K. Waltke, Ed.) (electronic ed.) (443). Chicago: Moody Press.

*Laurita writes:*

*I have found (to my extreme embarrassment) that shame is hardwired, but, like any component of the yetzer ha-ra it can be re-directed, re-programmed, overwritten, perverted, or paved over. Embarrassment is composed of magnetic elements, and it can be polarized to ANYTHING that I have determined to be a ruler over me. The Cross is a source of shame for me; I am furiously, overwhelmingly embarrassed before the Throne and before the universe that it has happened because of me. It is the most embarrassing thing that has ever happened to me, and I would have it so for all eternity. When I choose to have This Man to rule over me, I accept the shame of that Cross as mine. To not confess my sin is to deny it, however. The Cross does not bother me as long as I am not sorry! When I am magnetized to the god of this world, however, I have polarized myself to its rule. Self wants to have all the results of love, but it wants them from another source. Self wants the approbation of others, but Self wants that more than it wants the approbation of G-d. Fear of man is the deepest, most pervasive fear we have (no, sorry spiders, you can only scare us; you cannot make us embarrassed!). When I suffered from that fear, anything that I did (or did not do), I automatically calculated against the potential fear factor of What Would Others Think. Now, like breathing or not stepping out in front of trucks, that is not a bad thing. We were made to care about what others think! Where the problem comes in for me is when I make a decision that what others think is MORE IMPORTANT than what G-d thinks. At that point, I have established another god. Saul gave Samuel an excuse when Samuel found out that he had not completely obeyed the instructions he had been given after he had won the victory over the Amalekites. Saul said "I feared the people". Now, to me, that was Saul's sin. He put the opinion of others above the plain instructions of YHVH.*

*Sadly, I find that my ability to be ashamed can be perverted; it can be used to make me sin; it can also hold me in bondage after I have sinned, too. Embarrassment is a flesh response, and, like all other flesh responses, is not safe for me until I have handed it over to be redeemed; transformed and brought under subjection to Yeshua, and specifically, to Him on that Cross. The Cross has to be more embarrassing to me than anybody or anything else in this world. I have to be conformed to where I am with my Savior up and above where I am conformed to where I am at with anybody else. They did not die to save me from death, so I must not allow Fear of Others to kill me with embarrassment UNLESS I have run my sin through the filter of the Law Giver hanging there for me, first. I have learned this to my sorrow. I cannot confess my sin, my transgression of His Law, to others, TO KEEP FROM confessing it to Him. When I do confess to Him, first; then, and only then, is it safe to blush in front of others!*

*Evil controls vast numbers of people through Fear of Man. We are warned of this in Proverbs 29:25, where the snare that the fear of man brings is contrasted with the trust we should have put in the Lord instead. I used that unqualified trust in others as a guide in the places I was not putting my trust in Him. Invariably, I would find myself in*

47

*compromising positions, crawling with embarrassment; fractured and framed. Snared. One of the funniest examples of what that snare can look like is where, in Matt. 21, Yeshua's authority was being questioned. The chief priests and elders, in fact were trying to embarrass Him. They assumed He suffered from the Fear of Man, like they did, but He, knowing that they did, turned it around and asked them about whether they thought the baptism of John was from heaven, or of men. It is telling that they did not say it was of men because they FEARED THE PEOPLE.*

*Paul asks in Gal. 1:6 "...do I seek to please men? for if I yet pleased men, I should not be the servant of Christ." Heb. 13:5, 6 gives me the most definitive understanding of what order of operations I should establish in my life. The writer quotes "..."I will never leave thee, nor forsake thee (the basis for my trust in Him)." So that we may BOLDLY SAY, The Lord is my helper, and I will not fear what man shall do unto me."*

*When I repented for Fear of Man (and that included fear of my own opinion, too!) as the idolatry that it is, and submitted myself back to G-d as the only Source for my trust, I found I received an amazing gift in return. I found that I was then free to blush for all the right reasons! No longer bound by shame and frozen by fear, I was free to be humble, and free to admit my mistakes without dying on the spot! (Still learning this, y'all!) I have discovered that I can apologize without making others uncomfortable from this place, but, best of all, the evil in others can no longer control me in my shame! What a bonus! Free to blush! Who knew I had to be*

48

*delivered to do that, too! When I am obedient and put ALL THINGS under subjection to Yeshua, including what my reaction is to what others may think of me, I am free from their sin as well as mine. Then, and only then, do I find that shame works for me, instead of against me! Hallelujah!*

**8.** *"I, even I, am the one who wipes out **your** transgressions for My own sake, And I will not remember your sins."* Isaiah 43:25 NASB

## Personal Pronoun

"Centuries of Christian usage have accustomed readers of the New Testament to think of 'forgiveness' as primarily a gift to the individual person, which can be made at any time. It is, in that sense, abstract and ahistorical, however much it may burst upon one's consciousness with fresh delight in particular historical situations. On this basis, analyses of Jesus' offer of forgiveness have tended to focus on the piety (the *sense* of forgiveness) or the abstract theology (the *fact* of forgiveness, or the belief in it) of Jesus' hearers and/or the early church. The entire argument of this book so far indicates that this puts the cart before the horse. What is regularly missing from analyses of forgiveness is that which, arguably, stands front and center in precisely those biblical and post-biblical Jewish texts upon which Jesus and the early church drew more heavily. *Forgiveness of sins is another way of saying 'return from exile.'*"[10]

The suffixed pronoun, *ka*, to the noun *peša'*, resulting in the translation "*your* transgressions," doesn't indicate the referent of the pronoun. But the referent is crucial. It is *not* you and me. *It is Israel*, the nation of the elect, the entire constituency of the children of YHVH. N. T. Wright's observation resets the entire stage of our egocentric concern

---

[10] N. T. Wright, *Jesus and the Victory of God*, p. 268.

with forgiveness.  YHVH forgives—*Israel*—at a time when He restores the Kingdom to the earth. *Then* the nation will know the rightouesness of YHVH.  *Then* the people will see the holiness of their God and experience His Torah pouring forth from Zion.  *Then* the Messiah will turn over the Kingdom to the Father.  *Then* our burdens will be lifted and full fellowship will become a reality.

But until then, we breathe Babylon—and choke on the air.

If we are going to pursue a life of righteousness, we will need more motivation than "doing the right thing," a culturally dependent motive easily circumvented in the face of emotional desires.  We will need more than morality to survive the *tsunami* of excuses and approvals that Babylon offers.  Even the truth of wounding the heart of YHVH may not be enough to overcome long-established patterns of self-protection.  Perhaps that's why Wright's comment is so important.  Forgiveness is a God-act, and it isn't complete until *God* removes Babylon. Yes, we as individuals can experience the blessing of acquittal.  Yes, we can know grace as salve for the soul.  But in the end, sin will surround until *God* acts to remove its presence.

If you wondered why, once forgiven, you continue to fight, sometimes losing your grip on the righteousness you so desperately need, now you know.  We wait for God.  We wait in anticipation of the day when Israel, all Israel, will at last be home. Day 8.

*Laurita writes:*

*And just who are the 144,000 of Revelation 14, who are successfully keeping the "commandments of God and the faith of Jesus"? Are they not the perfected Body of the saints, signified by the perfect formation 12 x 12 and a thousand deep, of a Body who has finally gotten it figured out, and can finally show the world what obedience is, and how to do it, and that it CAN BE DONE? And HOW are they doing those commandments of G-d? The verse tells us: with the faith of Yeshua, and not their own. They have learned how to light the holy fire with His Spirit, and not with sparks of their own kindling. They have given up on might and power, as those have always been the methods of righteousness (law) that the world is forced to employ, and have learned (perfected) the way of the Spirit, and no, I don't think that means that they stayed in church all week laying on the floor!*

*Is not the Kingdom come when the Law has been perfected in the subjects, and will they not be the executors of righteousness when their obedience has been fulfilled? Has not the accusation of ha-satan from the Garden on been that the requirements of G-d are impossible to keep, but did not Yeshua come to return to us the power that enables us to do that? Unforgiven sin weakens me. Guilt cuts me off at the knees. Shame makes me an easy prey. Fear; that fear that is a side effect of the insanity that attempting to follow a lie always engenders, is the biggest source of weakness of all. I have no defense against any of this weakness in my flesh. All I can do, in an attempt to limp along sideways, is to cut miserable deals with the devil, and therefore align myself under the banner of the*

52

*other kingdom. But G-d! He came to give back to
me the keys of His glorious Kingdom of complete
power, and those keys consist of the Rock of my
Salvation and His Holy Spirit. Hallelujah!*

*What is the Kingdom of Israel? Is it a certain rocky
hill? Is it a certain genetic structure? Is it a certain
attainment of political identity? Who is Israel? And
how is this kingdom determined? Is this not a
Kingdom defined by the subjects, and are not the
subjects defined by their own choices? And is the
choice of obedience really possible, or is it not?
Revelation seems to think that it is. On thing is for
sure, obedience is not going to be possible until the
disobedience has been repented and forsaken. And
forgiven. And that, my friends, is something that I
think we are going to have to learn how to seek
together, as the replacement for disobedience,
which is relationship, is the thing we should have
been already doing instead anyway. So am I
praying for the conviction and forgiveness of those
around me, and actively pursuing the freedom of
others or not; or is evangelism just a dirty word
these days, and something that only the Apostles
did? Do I care that others around me are in the
boat with me, or do still I think that it is all just
about me? Can I really learn how to think and act
as a collective organism? The kingdom of Self says
"NO", but is that the kingdom I am supposed to be
lining up under?*

**9.** *"For this reason I say to you, her sins, which are many, have been forgiven, for she loved much; but he who is forgiven little, loves little."* Luke 7:47 NASB

## Measuring Stick

All or just a lot? That's the question with the Greek adjective *polli*. Is the use of this word in the gospel inclusive (all) or exclusive (some)? First we need to know the difference. If "much" is inclusive, then it is describing everything included in the idea. For example, "the many people" means *all* the people. But an exclusive use of the adjective has the sense of *some* of a greater number, for example, when we describe many pilgrims, but not *all* pilgrims, made a trip to Jerusalem. Here's the interesting fact. Hebrew has no plural word meaning "all." Therefore, the Hebrew use of "much" or "many" is virtually always *inclusive*. Whatever is described means everything.

Yeshua wasn't speaking Greek to Simon the Pharisee. He was speaking Hebrew, so his use of "much" in Hebrew (translated in Luke into the Greek *polys*) must mean *all*, not just some. *All* of her sins were burdening her. *All* of her sins have been forgiven. As a result, *all* of her is expressed in her act of love. The sweep of grace captures everything. There are no crumbs of disobedience left on the table or fallen to the floor.

But when grace does not clean the table, when some crumbs are held back, then the appropriate expression is not "some" of the whole but rather "little," a comparative term suggesting miserly appropriation of what was actually available.

Thus, the measuring stick. *"All in"* is the true measure of love. Bet everything. Take the full risk. Put it all on the line. Whatever is held back is a sure sign of comparative self-protection and, more importantly, a lack of trust in the graciousness of God. He is willing to include everything. The real question is whether *we are willing*.

The perplexing psychological twist of human righteousness is that it is generally *exclusive*. It operates like this: "I'm really not that bad. I'm generous. I'm industrious. I'm pretty responsible. I have high standards. Sure, I don't always meet them, but then, who does? I'm not perfect. So, yes, I need forgiveness—*for those things I can't seem to manage myself.*" In other words, we have the propensity to appropriate God's offer *exclusively*, that is, as applied only to those things we can't deal with ourselves. But that's not how grace works. Grace is *inclusive*. It washes *all of me*, not just those parts that I think need forgiving. Grace is a complete overhaul. That's why Isaiah, realizing the inclusiveness of grace, can say: "For all of us have become like one who is unclean, and all our righteous deeds are like a filthy garment; and all of us wither like a leaf, and our iniquities, like the wind, take us away" (Isaiah 64:6). He understood the scope of grace could not be limited to what *I* think is the problem. The problem is *me! All of me!* And all of me is in need of grace, which, fortunately, YHVH is willing to provide—on an "all in" scale.

Once we confront our true sinfulness, once we recognize that all our pretenses to self-justification and self-righteousness are just as much an issue as our clear moral failures, then we are ready to love much because then we will understand that we have been forgiven right down to the bottom of our toes. Day 9.

*Laurita writes:*

*I cannot come to the altar, with my mostly-good self(!), and offer the little I have done wrong(!) to be forgiven. No, a little leaven leavens the whole lump. That is what Passover teaches me. All of the 'right' thing, but done in the wrong spirit; just a slight bobble on the delivery of an impressive exercise; a mere misinterpretation of the true intent of an interaction, and, voila! the whole thing has to be scrapped! Start-over time for me!*

*No, when I mess up, all of me was there on the scene of the crime; all of me got dirty, too. All of me is responsible when any of me didn't make it to the other bank. So what if I jumped the river, but fell in a foot from the bank? All of me got wet!*

*When I repent, all of me must do so, too. Further, when I have broken even a little bit of the Law, it is if I had broken it all. I read an impressive story once about a truly brilliant guy who scoffed at keeping the Sabbath. He boasted that he was a good person, and that the Sabbath was just an outdated afterthought. An old Sabbath-keeper confronted him on it, and told him that if he was breaking one part of the Law, he was guilty of it all. He volunteered to prove it to him. Then, he proceeded to walk him through all the other nine, and show him that, in the process of ignoring the one, he was having to employ the breaking of all the other nine to do it. He made his case, and won the man.*

*The Law must all hang together, for it is woven out of one piece of fabric, like the veil that hung in front of the Holy of Holies. To rip one part, then, is to rip it all. There is no conceivable way, then, that I am ever going to be able to walk around with my head held high because I am 'good enough'. No, grace is the only way that all of me is going to be free, because otherwise, none of me is free as long as any of me is still trapped in the burning building. A Get Out Of Jail pass is not the same thing as saying that I didn't do the crime! Skating on grace. Only one thing makes it possible. ALL of me has to pretty much stay camped out at that altar! Like, all the time! The only way to avail myself of that grace is to look into that Law of liberty on a continual basis, so as to repent before that altar for what isn't being reproduced in my life yet. That is like, not there yet, ya'll! (Um, you can find my camping-out booth down the second row, third from the right...)*

**10.** *For the Lord God is a sun and shield; the Lord gives **grace** and glory; no good thing does He withhold from those who walk uprightly.* Psalm 84:11 NASB

## Face time

Day 10. We have taken time to examine ourselves. We put aside some of our theological constrictions in order to *feel* the heart of God. We wept the bitter tears of our self-righteous presumptions. We came face-to-face with the measuring stick. We faced the enemy culture that surrounds us and that fed us for so many years. We anticipate the final day of deliverance. With all of this in mind, now we need favor—His favor—to wash over us and make us clean. We need to know *hanan*.

Grace is not a theological concept in Hebrew. That might be hard to grasp. We are so used to grace as an *idea* that we fail to realize it is first and foremost a *quality* in the ancient Semitic world. In other words, grace is "a term of beauty" that describes "an aesthetically pleasing presentation of aspect of someone or something" that makes a "pleasing impression."[11] What's most important is this: in the Tanakh "only Yahweh is ever said to be able to give favor."[12] *Hanan*, "grace" or "favor" is a divine prerogative. YHVH gives *hanan*. *He finds something pleasing in us!* This idea is radically different than the theology we grew up with, a theology that convinced us that there was *nothing*

---

[11] D. L. Freedman and J. R. Lundbom, *hanan*, TDOT, Vol. V, p. 22.
[12] Ibid., p. 23.

about us that would or could please God. We were convinced by men like Augustine and Luther than being human meant being *wrong*. Remember Pedro Calderon de la Barca [look here if you don't: (http://skipmoen.com/2014/05/19/madness/)]? Why try if we are *doomed* to fail. Madness. But this is not the way YHVH views us. He is filled with *hanan* and *hanan* is incompatible with punishment.

"Favor cannot coexist with judgment. It is given or withdrawn according to whether one is positively disposed toward another. . . Love can coexist with judgment (Prov. 3:12) and exists at a deeper level of the inner consciousness, where conflicting emotions are allowed to coexist." [13] But Freedman and Lundbom's first point is crucial. *Hanan* is a function of *God's disposition* toward us, not our evaluation of our worthiness before Him. He *chooses* to show us favor because *He finds something pleasing in us*, not because we find something worthy in us.

We have examined our sins and our penchant toward relinquishing control to the *yetzer ha'ra*. We know we deserve our fate. But our evaluation *is not a factor in God's favor*. His love does bring judgment and for that we should be eternally grateful. Judgment alters the course of life. But His *favor*, His grace, does *not* depend on what we think of ourselves. And for that we must rejoice. All of the guilt we inherited from mistaking grace for love is washed away with the same cleansing that carries off our disobedience. Perhaps this is even more valuable than the declaration of acceptance. It

---

[13] Ibid., p. 24.

doesn't matter if we are convinced we are miserable failures before the Holy One of Israel. He has chosen to look upon us with favor.

*Laurita writes:*

*I have been spending the morning contemplating the parsha focus on the Nazarite vows, and that at the completion of them the Nazarite was to bring a sin offering. For what? For abstaining from what G-d had blessed; namely, the fruit of the vine, among other things! I truly wonder what the mainstream would think of this – not that I have seen them ponder it!*

*This understanding that we are to operate out of blessing; plenty; fullness; a serotonin and endorphin (pleasure pathway) reality instead of an adrenaline one, where ALL our strength is to be found in His joy, and NONE of it is to be found in our lack (shame, fear, worry and anxiety, GUILT, et al) goes straight up against the pagan grain of noble(!) sacrifice; death; beating about the face and body; vows of chastity, poverty and general lack as a PATHWAY to 'perfection'.*

*Most all living fauna, it seems, all the way down to the humble single celled bacteria, have serotonin receptors built into the surface of their cell structures. WHY? Because all creatures were created to learn through pleasure, and avoid through pain! We repeat what we found felt good last time because we were created that way! And it was pronounced good; very good! Paganism must employ force, however, (because they don't have access to the Love Channel!). We are perverted, not because we want what feels good, but because we want it in the wrong way, at the wrong time, through the wrong channels, and also because those pathways can be subverted or hijacked. I have found that Torah, through its emphasis on bridling the entire composite organism that we are; experience of body, as well as mind and soul, is designed to keep us (or bring us!) into alignment with the correct response to pleasure, specifically. Look at the Scripture: it is full of references to our entire experience as being designed for all things marvelous, tasty, mind-blowingly glorious (but simultaneously peaceful). Hello! No pain in sight! Pain was designed to show us where NOT to be. Hmm.*

**11.** *A good name is more desirable than great riches;* **to be esteemed** *is better than silver or gold.* Proverbs 22:1 NIV

## God's Business

For ten days we have examined the emotional climate of our rebellion. We discovered that YHVH accepts our self-serving criticism and casts it aside in an act of pure favor (*hen*). We recognized that we contribute nothing to His decision. We don't merit what He willingly bestows. But He nevertheless determines to love us—and to act in ways that will bring about an acknowledgment and acceptance of that love, even in self-inflicted disparagement. In other words, grace (*hen*) is a gift.

Now we are quite used to the expression "grace is a gift from God," but in all likelihood we have failed to realize just how monumental this action really is. According to the analysis of Fabry, because *hen* truly is a gift, it must be requested. "It is freely given and cannot be grasped or seized by force. The giver has every right to withhold his *hen*, and unless he is a person of rank, this may be done even at some risk. For the one receiving *hen*, this gift is unlike most in that it never really becomes his possession. One quite literally finds favor in the eyes of another, and this is where the favor remains."[14]

Let's examine this relationship for a moment. What

---

[14] D. L. Freedman and J. R. Lundbom, *hanan*, TDOT, Vol. V, p. 26.

Fabry notices is that favor is dynamic. It exists only insofar as the benefactor provides it. Favor is never actually passed to the recipient. It cannot be demanded, commanded or earned. Because it is the gift of the benefactor, it always remains within the power of the benefactor. In other words, grace is *never yours*. It is always a function of the *dynamic relationship between God and you*. If we think of salvation, the product of grace, in this way, we will realize that the experience we have of "being saved" is in fact the experience of God's granting us His favor which He alone provides, on His terms and according to His desire. This entails that our estimation of worthiness is totally irrelevant to the act. And it also entails that grace is God's business alone. If He deems to grant you and me favor, it's His business, and nothing that we did can undo His act. It is, of course, possible that we might spurn this act and it is equally possible that He might withdraw it, but insofar as God alone determines His acts of favor, His promise not to abandon His children, not to count their inequities against them any longer, not to destroy them, is an eternal decision, independent of the evaluation of their worthiness (or unworthiness).

This is enormously good news. If it were up to us, we would never find rescue from our damaged state. Why? Because we know all too well the catalogue of our failures. Our own internal sense of justice would demand retribution. But God is not a man, and He doesn't act as men would act. He has determined to rescue us, and that determination *is all that matters*. Our careful evaluation of unworthiness *does not affect His decision* to show favor. Therefore, it should not affect our willingness to embrace His favor.

This verse in Proverbs speaks directly to our need to re-evaluate our self-hatred. Although disguised in translation, the Hebrew text actually says "_hen_ is better than silver and gold." It is *favor* that really matters—and God has given it.

Who are we to refuse? Day 11.

*Laurita writes:*

*Skip has made several good points. If grace is a true gift, it has to be asked for. What? Why? If grace is unmerited favor, than why is it not just bestowed in one grand, blanketing, one-size-fits-all maneuver? He also observes that there is a relationship between "willingness to embrace His favor" and "our need to evaluate our self hatred". Everything that stands in the way of me experiencing the full impact of grace in my life is generated by me; originates on my side of the ledger, and therefore, is up to ME to do something about. What? Why? Because grace is a done deal on G-d's part; there is nothing more He can do because He has already done it all! Therefore, the world should have already cashed in this get-in-free ticket: this deal should have already been consummated. Why has it not been? Because we simply don't, won't believe it! Why not? Because when we worship self, which we all do, we HAVE to believe that at least SOMETHING good must originate with us; we have to have at least some part of the credit. Grace, by its very definition, tells me that there isn't even a ghost of a chance that*

*that is possible. SomeOne Else already evaluated the situation and concluded that it is hopeless for us to even try to gain merit. So much for my self-esteem!*

*Y'all, I am going to tell you a dirty little secret: we don't know what love is! Yep, if you go ask a person in the flesh to tell you what love is, we are all going to think we do, but none of us are going to get it right. Why? It comes from the fact that we are all, either overtly or covertly, worshiping ourselves; and further, because all of us think that because we worship ourselves, we (naturally!) are loving ourselves. We were created to think that way, in fact, so don't go beating yourself up about it. Just sayin'. In fact, I think we assume that the two must be a tautology (saying the same thing). And because we think that, we will proceed to lay out how we actually treat ourselves in that worship as a demonstration of what love is. We get our definition of love from whatever we experience that we THINK is love. If I think I love myself, then I am going to assume that the way I am actually treating myself must be love. And I am going to be wrong! Guaranteed!*

*I worship all that I fear. I fear all that I perceive has power over me. I grant power over me to everything that I look to satisfy my needs. My needs are generated by a surfeit of love in those places; my needs show me WHERE I should be relating with G-d, self, others, or the cosmos in general. My needs, then show me where I am, literally, 'not in touch (relationship)' with reality! When I grant myself the power to satisfy my own need for love (the world's definition of self love), I then assume*

65

*that I actually CAN do that! The reality, of course, is vastly different. I am not a source of love. Because I am not, I have set myself up to fail at loving myself enough to satisfy ALL my need to be related and connected to everything and everyone at all levels. Whew! No wonder I am failing myself! And, folks, as creatures hardwired for love, we hate everyone and everything that fails to deliver that love. (Even G-d does!) I hate myself as a natural consequence, then, of looking to myself for something I must have, but cannot provide.*

*The biggest thing; the ONLY thing, between me and the grace of G-d, then, is ME. I will not, cannot, know His grace unless and until I have surrendered my rebellious establishment of my Self as a rival for the love He offers. I cannot worship G-d and my Self: I cannot establish both as a source for love in my life. Until I repent for what I THOUGHT was self-love (it was not; true self love is a derivative of relationship with a true Source for that love), I will never have the room in my life to receive His love. Here lies the paradox of sin. Sin is a TWISTING of the truth: it takes the WORDS of truth, and perverts the meaning and the application. I must repent for believing the twisting. I believed I knew what love was, and that I could provide it for myself. My sin was that I did not take His Word for what love was, and take Him as my Source for that love. Why did I not do that?*

*Sin lies to me with fear, and says that I must avoid all that I fear, which is a perversion of the way I was made. I was made to fear only what would hurt me, and I was made to only hurt when I messed up. If I start from myself as a source of love, however, I will turn all that fear, hurt, and hatred in the wrong direction. Here is where I need the Comforter. I need courage from beyond myself to face that fear and that self-hatred. I must wade back through all that mess and insanity that I have made of myself because I did NOT know what love was. Fear says "run!" "hide!", but fear that is based on a lie must be called out and faced.*

*Grace was offered because my mess – my response to my need for love – is hopeless, but until I face the mess, I cannot repent that mess, and until I repent that mess, I cannot trade it in for that grace. Grace does not invite me away from my mess; grace invites me THROUGH my mess. This is why I think the world has not taken G-d up on His offer. We all want to be saved in our sins, or in spite of our sins, but the only thing that is offered is salvation FROM our sins. What is sin? A fracture point in relationship. What is grace? An offer to restore those relationships. How will I experience that grace? Y'all, I have to become willing to show back up at those fracture points (which is what repentance IS). Sin is where I ran from relationship; grace gives me another chance for relationship in three dimensions: with G-d, self and others, but I am the one who has to become willing to try again. How will I know if grace has shown up in my life? Well, grace shows up when I do!*

*I would like to recommend Skip's book, The Lucky Life as a good, fresh look at this subject. (Thank you, George Kraemer, for loaning it to me, and Skip for writing it!)*

**12.** *I shall **delight** in Your statutes; I shall not forget Your word.* Psalm 119:16 NASB

## Mesillat Yesharim

Moses Luzzatto published *Mesillat Yesharim* in 1740. His insights into the relationship between righteous acts, joy and obligation are just as important today as they were two hundred and fifty years ago. Luzzatto argued that human beings are driven by the pursuit of pleasure, the impulse to find ultimate joy in living. There is nothing wrong with this desire. In fact, without it life would be meaningless. Life's big question is to define the proper object of this pursuit. According to Luzzatto, joy is achieved through the pathway of the commandments. They are designed to bring human beings into the presence of the divine, and according to Scripture, this is ultimate joy. We may be distracted by all kinds of other substitutes, and certainly the world offers them on a daily basis, but true joy, joy that fills our souls to the brim, is found in the experience of God's graciousness and abiding presence. This is what makes us really human and it is this that every one of us seeks. Once tasted, nothing else will do.

But Luzzatto makes a crucial observation. "For this world is the only place where the *Mizvot* can be observed. Man is put here in order to earn with the means at this command the place that has been prepared for him in the world to come. In the words of our Sages, 'This day is intended for the observance of the *Mizvot*; the morrow, for the enjoyment of the reward earned by means of them.'"[15]

Before you raise theological objections to the idea of "earning" a place in the *olam ha'ba*, consider the greater impact of Luzzatto's observation. Ira Stone's commentary makes it clear.

1. "the goal of achieving joy expresses itself through the commandments."
2. "the idea that joy comes to us in the form of commandments is counterintuitive,"
3. "there is neither perfection nor addition after death."
4. "that state in which man departs will remain with him for eternity."
5. "one who becomes a blot on the face of God does so only in this world and can rectify that situation only in this world."[16]

John the Baptist said the same thing. "Repent, for the kingdom of heaven is at hand." Yeshua echoed the same thought. Today is the day of salvation. Today is the day that we enter into the grace (favor – *hen*) of the Lord. What is done today brings us closer to joy. What is not done today will remain with us for eternity.

Now we know why David uses the word *sha'ah* in his poem. He delights (*sha'ah*) in the commandments because the commandments are the way to joy. Without them, ethical behavior devolves into personal opinion (see my analysis here: http://skipmoen.com/2013/10/27/pillars-of-

---

[15] Moses Hayyim Luzzatto, *Mesillat Yesharim*, p. 17.
[16] Ibid., Stone's commentary in various remarks pp. 17-25.

heaven-the-ethical-dilemma-of-religion-without-torah/). But with them, you and I can know the way to God's heart and we discover that the favor He poured out upon us has a purpose, to provide us with the motivation to direct that inherent pursuit of ultimate joy toward Him.

Let's not be foolish. We are grateful for forgiveness, but gratitude is not enough motivation to overcome temptation when joy is at stake. As human beings, we desperately desire to live satisfied and satisfying lives. What presents itself as a means of achieving that goal is powerful — sometimes so powerful that we overlook the commandments and ignore their demands simply because we need emotional care. The more we hurt, the more we seek the goal of ultimate joy. Each slice of satisfaction we are able to feel increases our desire for more. God knows all this. He promises that the way of the righteous, *mesillat yesharim*, the way of Torah, will bring us the kind of joy we truly desire. He promises, but we do not always believe Him.

Our problem is not ignorance of the Way. Our problem is not reticence on the part of the Divine. Our problem is not lack of motivation. Our problem is *trust*. If we trust His promises, He gives us ample instruction to achieve the goal we really desire. If we do not trust His promises, we are left to devise ways to achieve that goal without Him. And all of this struggle can be worked out only here, only now. When it comes to this issue, the issue of trust, there is no tomorrow. Day 12.

*Laurita writes:*

*Amen. It seems to me that there is no faith in the world to come: the angels know nothing of faith. There is no room left for faith when we are face to face. At that point, reality is overwhelming. Much as I complain about the seeming lack of underpinning for my relationship with the Unseen and Unknown, if He were any more present at all, I would have no room left to choose Him. Without faith it is impossible to please Him, however – for me, anyway. Other creatures, who exist to do His pleasure, are in a different position of choosing, for sure. My love is demonstrated by my being, literally, free to choose Him. Or not. That is something that is simply not possible in His Presence. The tremendous strength of will involved in that covering cherub's actually accomplishing that, could have only been possible in the thick darkness surrounding that Throne. Somehow, enough was a mystery, was not revealed, where it was still possible to have a choice based on trust. I cannot read minds. If I could, trust would no longer be possible; I would already know. If I were just part of some amorphous stream or cloud of consciousness, there would be no individuality left; no ME left; no position of personal probability left as a launching pad for trust. Love must have trust, but trust is only possible under certain conditions. You said "When it comes to this issue, the issue of trust, there is no tomorrow." Now is the day of our salvation. Today, harden not your hearts. Tomorrow may never come. When I am already wrong, only grace can set me back on the track, the Way, but grace is only possible where I still have*

71

*freedom of choice. To be free to choose, I have to be able to trust; but to be able to trust, there has to be elements that have not been revealed. Yet. If I need to know it all up front, before I whip out my checkbook, I run the risk of "ever learning, but never coming to the truth." At some point, I must learn how to jump. I cannot wait until Next Time to get that one down. I have to learn free fall here. Now. Trust. "I'm jumping, Daddy. Catch me! Whee!" The joy of the Lord can only be the exhilaration of sheer trust. Thrill seekers, eat your heart out! Trust is hardcore fun!*

**13.** *The sins which pass **unnoticed** beset a man on the Day of Judgment.* Avodah Zarah 18a

## *What Didn't Matter Before*

"Hypocrisy and rationalization transform the tokens of religious life from sources of grandeur to sources of shame." [17] Stone goes on to suggest that worshipping God in a state of "uncleanness" is worse than not worshipping Him at all.

How did we get into this despicable state in the first place? We certainly did our best to clean up those deliberate acts of disobedience. We might have struggled to remove some habitual sin, to live a "moral" life. But then we discover upon more careful reflection that a good number of our actions are the result of simple cultural accommodation. They don't seem to be violations of God's delightful instructions because we have *become used to them.* But when we really look, we find that more often than not we are either excusing our behavior because it doesn't *seem* bad to us, or we are claiming the high ground but actually allowing cultural assumptions to rule the choices we really make.

The best, and most persistent, example of this rationalization and hypocritical behavior is *eating.* Our society put off the biblical requirements concerning food centuries ago. As a result, without actually thinking about what we are doing, we consume digestible products which the Bible does

---

[17] Ira Stone's commentary on Moses Luzzatto, *Mesillat Yesharim*, p. 108.

not consider food. And when our attention is drawn to this discrepancy, we either respond with an excuse or a rationalization. We cover up our sin with "common sense" and culture. The things that pass unnoticed will be revealed on the Day of Judgment, but then it will be too late to change.

I imagine that most of us have, at one time or another, attempted to come to terms with *kosher*. So perhaps "food" is no longer swept under the cultural carpet for you. But that doesn't mean there aren't other things—things that if you really stopped long enough to consider, you would realize that the source of their justification is not the Bible but rather the society. Perhaps how you dress, the words you use, the nearly automatic judgments you make about other people, the bias you show toward some, the assumptions you make about others, the way that you maneuver in order to achieve maximum success for yourself, the double standards you employ—all perfectly acceptable in the society but all suspect under the holiness of God. Things you don't usually even think about. Well, now is the time to think about them.

What actions and attitudes have you rationalized as "not really being that bad"? What have you habitually done and found ample excuses for doing? How do you take care of yourself in ways that you know might be on the edge of righteousness but don't cause waves in the culture? Once we embark on the pathway toward holiness, most if not all of our common behaviors will have to come under scrutiny—now or then. Better now. Day 13.

*Laurita writes:*

*What if the 'little things' ARE the big things? What if we get it all right like Martha (who was concerned for the temporal necessities) but in the process, we neglect to get it right like Mary (who was focused on the spiritual necessities)? What if I do ALL the rules, but do them for the wrong reasons? What if the wrong spirit actuates right actions? What if I say "sorry" like a little kid with gritted teeth and murder in his eye, or show up at church just because I wanted others to think something of me? What if I took all the baths at all the right times, but did it for the purpose of making it impossible to determine on the surface the filthiness of the accusing thoughts of others; the judgment, the superiority, the indulgence of the essential competition we all seem to think we must engage in to 'get ahead'? What if I followed all the rules SO AS TO 'get ahead' (what does that mean? Does get ahead mean that others must be behind?) What if I got all the "Lord, Lord's" right, just to stand before the Throne and hear "depart from Me"?*

*And about that food. What if I ate all the right things, but about the time I figured I had it 'perfect' a spirit of self-congratulation showed up and made my prayer of thankfulness into hypocrisy? Would digesting it do me any good then?*

*Our culture is permeated from top to bottom with the wrong reasons for all the right things. We tout organic; natural; pure. Sure. Those are excellent. But in the flesh, even if we do manage to get the correct reason to do it (proper care of our body,*

76

*which is righteous), we must still employ wrong motivations, even if we manage to get the reasons in the ball park. I know eating right is good for me. The Law isn't the problem here. We can all agree that it is good. We should all take good care of our health. BUT, in the flesh, how do I overcome the secret self hatred I harbor in my life long enough to take that care? In secret, when I feel bad about myself, I turn to those carbs to raise my serotonin (which goes into the gutter the instant I agree with that self hatred). What does the world suggest? Why, employ the spirit of self hatred even more! It gives me all kinds of ways to beat myself up so as to get myself to do right. It gives me motivations like jealousy (shows me pictures of skinny people so I can want to be like them); accusation (you aren't doing it right!); unloving (you are not good enough); even altered states of reality (say this mantra, use this repetitive maneuver to 'trick' yourself), etc. ad nauseam. This is why the flesh can never do the Law. It has no power to overcome the sin that already exists in my life.*

*No, to do righteousness, I have to turn to a Source outside my sinful flesh for the power (freedom) to do it. There are powerful motivations for sin in my life already installed. I am already cursed with bondage. I am already fractured from myself, others and G-d. These fractures cause me, predispose me, to even more temptation. I know I should eat right. But, in areas of my life where fracture exists, and I don't feel connected, my serotonin levels reflect that fact, and, unless and until that fracture is fixed, I am going to have no natural resistance to carbs, or exercise even, or to using media or other substances to numb out or raise that serotonin, which I must have to live. The only answers the world has for this state is to temporarily rob Peter to pay Paul: I can use self hatred (adrenaline realities) to temporarily overcome my serotonin needs, but they will be back, and needier than before. No, the only way to get doing right is to be FREE to do it. Obeying the Law does not set me free (salvation from sin). No, I need to be saved from self hatred (delivered to love myself properly) BEFORE those serotonin levels are going to be high enough already that I no longer need those carbs, and thus am free to eat right. For the right reasons.*

*I would like to contend that righteousness (obeying the Law with a pure heart, which means rightly motivated, to me) is a SIDE EFFECT, if you will, of salvation. People sit there and worry all day long about the ultimate salvation of their souls, and about the Law, even, but can't seem to be bothered about the little things, like whether or not they are hating themselves right this minute, and need to whip into Krispy Kreme. I would like to humbly offer the thought that salvation only works when I avail myself of it, and that is a continual process. I have to repent for self hatred when I see it, and take my peace BEFORE I am free to obey. This is why I go through my life repenting. I have to be saved from my sin in each moment, before I am free to obey the Law.*

*To those who are struggling with the Law, may I say a few words? First, Someone died for you to save you from the death you already deserve. That blood was shed to cover all the stuff you haven't gotten to yet. All that is required of us is to work with the conviction that we have right now. He understands the rest. It is Greek to be obsessed with perfection. To me, it is Hebrew to realize that this is more like a cooperative dance, moment by moment. There is a reason that it is called a Way. The Way is not a thing I do to be free from sin. No, the Way is a person I dance with after He frees me from bondage. The Law does not come separate from its Giver! Hallelujah!*

**14.** *"The second is this: 'Love your neighbor as yourself.' There is no commandment greater than these."* Mark 12:31 NIV

## Motivation and Execution

It's Day 14. What a glorious day! For a dozen sessions, we have examined our true state of self-protection. We found something vitally important. God's favor (*hen*) is *God's* business. It does not depend on our evaluation of worth. That's a very good thing since we know we don't measure up. If we are going to find true joy in this world, then God not only provides the foundation (grace) but also the means (Torah). We may begin this process motivated by gratitude, but we can continue the process only when we realize that the goal is more than gratitude. It is self-fulfillment. We sustain our pursuit of righteousness because it satisfies *us*.

Great! We are rescued from inner self-hatred. We are set on the path toward satisfaction. We are motivated by our internal pursuit of joy. What else do we need? Ah, we need to know *how* to make this happen. It's not enough to be pushed out of the nest. We must be taught how to fly. And for that we are provided with the second great commandment—Love your neighbor as yourself. You see, ultimately we want to achieve the goal of the first great commandment. We want to love God with all our hearts, minds and strength. Why? Because then we will experience His presence and experience true joy. But how do we go about loving God with everything? Do we sequester ourselves from all of life's distractions? Do we devote ourselves to Torah study? Do we attend services daily? Yeshua cites Leviticus 19:18 in order to provide further direction. We love God with all we have by loving our neighbors in the same way we care for ourselves.

Actually, this isn't a new thought. The word *hen* already contains this idea. "Benevolence is an act of grace shown by the rich toward the poor, or at least by an individual with means toward one who has little or no means. . . Therefore, the generous person is *tsaddiq*, 'righteous.' . . . Generally speaking, someone who is gracious to the *'ani* will be happy (Prov. 14:21). But more important is the knowledge that showing grace to the needy honors Yahweh (Prov. 14:31)."[18] Exodus 34:6-7 shows us that YHVH is full of *hen*; that *hen* is a central attribute of His character. When we act as He would act, we honor Him and, *at the same time*, experience what it means to be in His presence. This is the reason that, for example, I consider my efforts to help the distressed community of Ranquitte, Haiti to build a road as one of the more important, and lovely, things I have ever done. Being part of loving these people whom I do not personally know by simply acting with benevolence toward them made me feel the presence of YHVH. Although that happened years ago, the memory of grace continues—and empowers.

Are you a sinner in need of grace? Certainly! Did YHVH show you His benevolence? Of course! Do you want to know Him with deeper intimacy? Ah,

---

[18] D. L. Freedman and J. R. Lundbom, *hanan*, TDOT, Vol. V, pp. 28-29.

then *love your neighbor*! Show benevolence toward someone in need. Do something for another. And God will show up. Day 14—the day we turn the corner.


*Laurita writes:*

*Thank you, Skip for preaching about sin/righteousness! And thank you that it is NOT titled "Sinners in the hand of an angry G-d" or "You're sunk before you start, so why try"! Or even titled "Once saved, always saved" or "Jesus did it all, so go home". No, we cannot cut ourselves out of equation, for good or for bad, but neither can we cut our Saviour out. Nope. It's together, all the way, like any good relationship.*

*How do you get close to someone else? Why, make an effort to love who they love, and be pleased by what they are pleased with. That's basic romance 101. In fact, if you have no desire to do that, there's a good chance you don't even love them. Or want to. "Do you love Me, Peter? Feed my sheep."*

*I was thinking yesterday about if I was given the choice of ONLY being able to love another, or have another love me – if I could not have both, then which one would I pick, and why? Yeshua knew the answer to this one when He preached, "It is more blessed to give than to receive". There are more rewards to loving, than being loved. The heart is satisfied better, and life's desires are more touchable. If I do not NEED, then I am stronger, too. Deals go down better, too, if I am more focused on what I bring to them than what I need from them. It is a stronger negotiating position. Needs are weaknesses; strength is where you say "take it or leave it; you are going to lose more than I if you walk away, and you are going to gain more if you stay". Irresistible line!*

*Basic order of operations in the Love Power Company: #1. Go to the Source. Get love. #2. Allow love (relationship) to apply to self (let the Source fill your tank). #3. Disseminate love (relate) to all others. When I do #3, I am sending what I got given back home to its Source, and, when I do that, the circuit is complete and the power lines are grounded: fully charged to do it again. I am just a plug on a route. If it stopped with me, it wouldn't even be able to start. I receive with the full intention of being able to turn around and share. I am only as rich as what I have to give. The widows of Zarephath and the Mite know: they were richest people in that whole Book! Richer than even Solomon, for sure. They knew the secret of true wealth. This is the wealth of the Kingdom. People who are still citizens of that Other kingdom would not want to migrate to this one. As long as I am focused on What's In It For Me, I don't want to hear about the blessings that are only gotten by participating in What's In It For Them. In fact, if you asked someone from the kingdom of Self to sit down and list all the conditions of what they think hell for them would be like, this one would surely top the list. No, the two kingdoms are opposites, and this is the dividing line -- the real litmus test, if you will. If I am not plugged into the Love of G-d, I have nothing to give. How do I plug in? Yeshua preached it: "REPENT, for the Kingdom of Heaven is at your hand". This one is up to me. I have to trade (repent) the poverty of my lack and fracture (focus on Self) before my hand is empty to receive the riches of relationship (The Law of Torah). "Repent and obey" sound like hell on earth to the flesh. I got news for the flesh: its even worse than that. They represent a death knell to the flesh. The two kingdoms are anathema to each other: Self sucks in; Love breathes out.*

**15.** *For the Lord God is a sun and shield; the Lord gives* **grace and glory***; no good thing does He withhold from those who walk uprightly.* Psalm 84:11 NASB

## Merit Badges

Ah, what we so desperately want! Joy. Joy of life. Joy of relationships. Joy that satisfies our deepest longings for acceptance, recognition, community. And YHVH promises this — and more. *Hen ve'kavod.* Favor and honor. Grace and glory.

But here's the rub. Not for everyone. *Hen ve'kavod* is promised to those who walk uprightly. "Prov. 3:4 teaches that keeping the commandments and practicing other virtues will give one *hen* in the eyes of God and human beings. The wicked person, says Isa. 26:10, should not be shown favor, for it will not help him earn righteousness. . . . This shows again that the OT has no aversion to merited favor."[19] So while we can set aside the idea that righteousness isn't earned (for in the context of the Semitic world it most certainly is), we are still left with an insurmountable obstacle. We are not righteous. In fact, we break the commandments – often, and as a result, we should not expect YHVH's favor. Grace is withheld. Joy is absent. All because we acted in ways that opposed His requests. What are we to do now? We see the ultimate object of our lives. It's there, hanging in the presence of the One true God, waiting to be grasped. But our hands are stained with the fruit of another tree, slippery with

---

[19] D. L. Freedman and J. R. Lundbom, *hanan*, TDOT, Vol. V, p. 31.

consumption of personal acquisition. And the real object lies just out of reach because we have moved just out of grasp.

If this were the end of the story, if measure-for-measure were the only scale in divine government, then who among us could ever be fulfilled?

There is only one hope. It is found in Numbers 23:19:

"God is not a man, that He should lie,
Nor a son of man, that He should repent;
Has He said, and will He not do it?
Or has He spoken, and will He not make it good?"

God is not a man. He is not bound by the ethical rules of men. He is not subject to our concepts of fairness, justice and governance. He is something entirely different. "The Lord, the Lord God, compassionate and gracious, slow to anger, and abounding in lovingkindness and truth;" (Exodus 34:6). God is not a man. He offers grace to the wicked—to you, to me. He erupts in kindness, mercy and _hesed_. _Hen_ is His middle name. Joy is possible, real, available—not because we have earned it but because it has been given. Then we go about learning to earn it. Day 15.

_Laurita writes:_

_It took me most of my life before I noticed that, in Psalm 23, goodness and mercy are the things that FOLLOW me. Why, I had been chasing that stuff all my life! But they are results: the aftereffects; not_ *primary causes; not goals to attain. I found that, in the process of trying to capture them, I had been chasing my tail, literally, most of my life. Why, they are supposed to be chasing me! They are the side effects of righteousness, if you will. When I reach out for Him, in all the ways He has given me to do that (and all the reaching, from repentance to longing, from trying and failing, to gratitude for all that He provided that I did NOT 'earn' – all, even the failing – is counted as righteousness – relationship), goodness and mercy are how He responds to me. There's no use trying to want the good stuff without Him, for He IS the good stuff. He cannot bless me without showing up, for there is no good thing apart from Him. It is a package deal, and this is why the wicked rage, for they want to commit highway robbery, and intercept the mail coach BEFORE it reaches the bank. They desire the good stuff without its Owner.*

*When I long for love, and attempt to reach out, He counts my pitiful attempts as the real thing, and does the rest. I am connected – which is what righteousness IS – ultimately, not because I am an expert at connecting, but because He met me, when I did try, ALL THE WAY. He gave me the motive force, He supplied the power to change, He even freed me up from the impotent bondage to sin so that I could choose and my choosing would actually result in something real; He met me all the way. He saw me when I was afar off and ran to meet me. I was stuck on the ledge, and He came and got me. AND, then, amazingly, He counted my miserable stuff as righteousness! Astounding!*

*I cannot get myself to the place where love goes down – where I can love and be loved – on my own. I have to repent for not being there, and accept the offer of a 'lift'. What is that lift? Why, I must leave behind my sins. I must be saved from fracture. How does that happen? I have to accept the invitation to, literally, be where He is, but where is He? On a cross. And He said that if He were lifted up, He would draw – would attract, would invite, us all. But I still have to accept the invitation. If I am to be saved FROM my sins, I have to crawl up there on that cross with Him, for repentance is where I take the responsibility back for my sins. I have to die to sin. I have to be crucified to my lusts. Self has to die so that the magnetic connection to the curse (death) that my sin (fracture) created can be broken. I have to die to live. He came to literally show me the Way to do that. Dying to self – how few know what that is! Self has to die before the true me can live. Sin has to go before I can be pure. I have to quit doing wrong before I can start doing right. I have to forsake the devotion to putting me first before I can start putting Him first. The correct order of operations is salvation, then obedience: repentance, then righteousness. As long as I think there is a ghost of a chance that I can 'earn' salvation, however, I am going to continue to get it backwards. What am I going to continue to forget up front? It is that I cannot choose obedience BEFORE repentance. I have to be sorry before I can be saved, and I have to be saved before I can be free. Free to do what? Obey. The children of Israel requested a three day journey into the wilderness so that they could obey their G-d. They had to be saved out of Egypt before they could get to Sinai. They had to quit being forced to make monuments to false gods before they could be free to worship the True One. I have to quit going the wrong way before I am able to turn around and head in the right direction. I am not going to be able to do right until I quit doing wrong. Hey, I am already fractured! No use pretending I ain't! I am already separated from goodness and mercy: forget the grace and glory! I have to be moving in the right direction (righteousness) before all that can show up in my life. I have to at least be wiggling so that He can show up to push and steer. Frozen in my sin, I need the shackles of my sins to be struck off before I am free to obey. Why do I need to be free? To obey. I need a Savior to put my feet on higher ground so that I can walk. Hallelujah! I have One!*

**16.** *Then the Lord passed by in front of him and proclaimed, "The Lord, the Lord God, compassionate and* **gracious***, slow to anger, and abounding in lovingkindness and truth;"* Exodus 34:6 NASB

## *"Joyful, joyful, we adore Thee"*

Sing it! Sing it loudly! This is not theology. This is freedom. This is rescue. This is the answer. Now, *how do you feel?*

"At Sinai, Yahweh introduced himself to Israel first and foremost as a God of grace."[20] Set aside the theological analysis of the *attributes* so commonly proof-texted with this verse. Remember the audience. Israel, recently enslaved to a god of power and vengeance, humiliated by the absence of divine protection, murdered without reprisals, subject to the whims of a pantheon of pagan deities, slowly absorbed into a world filled with hate, repression, apathy and abandonment. A world where the wicked prevail and those who attempt righteousness are summarily removed. Is YHVH's declaration a *theological* contention? Or is it an emotionally filled declaration of care, divine concern, stability for those whose lives were nothing but chaos?

---

[20] D. L. Freedman and J. R. Lundbom, *ḥanan*, TDOT, Vol. V, p. 33.

Sing it! "Joyful, joyful, we adore Thee." YHVH has made a way—a way for those too worn and battered to fight any longer, a way for those who compromised in order to survive, a way for the homeless, the frightened, the abused. A way no man could ever provide. The fact that this grace, this avenue to joy, comes on the rails of judgment does not diminish its beauty. Of course there must be judgment. How else will the grip of the Pharaohs of this world ever be defeated? We who have suffered under the taskmasters of our own folly, who have enslaved ourselves to the pursuit of what we could never find in the desert of wandering, are at last released. YHVH has spoken. Will He not fulfill what He has proclaimed?

For two weeks we have recounted the miseries of decades of life in search of peace—peace for ourselves, the tranquility of emotional confidence that we are enough, and peace for our world, the cooperation of the creation and the people who populate it in an anthem of praise for the One who brought us all to be. For two weeks we have listened to the heartbeat of despair, despair that we would ever see true forgiveness in a world no longer at war, in a life no longer malnourished. For two weeks we examined the feelings of those dark corners we have kept so carefully hidden. We have discovered that judgment, divine judgment of those things that have ravaged our lives, is the precursor to singing joyfully. Perhaps the lesson is simple: We cannot know the exuberance of joy without knowing the despair of disobedience. Deliverance only has meaning as the opposite of slavery.

Today, Day 16, is a day for remembering.

Remembering how we were rescued and what we were rescued from. Remembering that joy is the product of graceful judgment.


*Laurita writes:*

*"Deliverance only has meaning as the opposite of slavery." Hallelujah!*

*I spent most of yesterday thinking about what Michael C. wrote yesterday about Torah observance. He made the point that the Law is what we are saved INTO. It is the conclusion of salvation. In fact, if salvation does not dump me into the loving arms of that Law, then I have not been saved. Further, I have to be sorry, in order to be saved. Paul says that without the Law he would not have known what sin was. That gives me pause. Have I read the ENTIRE Law? Have I been sorry for EVERYTHING in it that I am not doing? Only the Law can show me what I must be saved from, and the Law is the only place I can go after I am. The Law provides the only place in the cosmos that I can be, and not be in sin. It is the only physical place of residence for me outside of sin. If salvation moves me, the Law provides the only place that I can be moved TO. It provides the only map for the escape route, because I do not know what I am to repent of without it, but it also provides my new home, for I have not repented (turned away from), if I have not simultaneously established obedience (turned toward), and the question then becomes, obedience to what? The Law hems me in: I cannot repent (the only basis for salvation) without it, and I have no other place to go after I am saved. Without*

94

*it, I am not, in fact, saved. There is no neutral hinterland, no limbo, out there that gives me a place to be where I am no longer in sin (saved) but not observing that Law.*

*It is grace that gives me everything to be thankful for, but freedom is what grace gives. There is no grace but what provides freedom. But, there is no freedom except from sin, and, because I suffer from the effects of sin every second of my life on this planet in some form or another, grace is what provides my only relief from that sin. It is by grace that I am not constantly (instantly) consumed in each moment, and that is even BEFORE I repent! Especially before! (Thank you, Yeshua! You died for me when I was still lost! That was grace, too!) Grace gives me what I would have had if I had been obedient in that place. Grace also puts me in a place of freedom where I can obey.*

*I think the world presumes much because of grace. The world concludes it must be doing 'all right' without G-d because they are 'living just fine' without Him! That is a breathtakingly presumptuous nose-thumbing at the grace that is providing that existence – that amazing chance (freedom) to choose again! So much of the gratitude I am rightly supposed to be walking in each moment must, by needs, come from being grateful for the goodness provided that is there IN SPITE OF my current disobedience. Grace keeps me humble and grateful. Grace gives me another chance to want to do better. Grace girds me behind and before, just as the Law does. In fact, there is no place I have been able to find where one is, and the other is not. They are two sides of one coin, and that coin is the only coin of the realm. If I make a move to spend grace to enter the Kingdom, I must needs employ the Law, too. Grace gives me a new chance to obey, but if I do not take that chance, I am still just as lost as if grace had not provided it. Grace provides all the reasons to jump for joy, but the physical space in creation to jump in; the very air my lungs has to breathe to shout with; is the freedom from sin that only the Law provides me. Grace is what dumps me back over the fence of that Law, out of sin, but then, I have to stay there! I am either sinning, or sorry for sinning, but I can only be sorry (repent, or, turn away FROM) if I have a place to turn away TO.*

*Only within the fence of Torah do I have a place to be joyful. There is a reason that David, in Psalm 119 (which is my favorite chapter in that whole Book), says the Law is what provides him all his delight. David has experienced the freedom of the fence. It is sin, and all its baleful effects, that is crushing the life out of me. Only within the Law can I find the love I so desperately need to live. Love can only exist within that fence, too, because the Law is what defines what love IS. Joy is what I experience when I have been set free: rescued from sin and its effects (curses) by grace from outside that fence, and returned to the love that can only be found within it. (May I stay there this time!) Hallelujah!*

**17.** *Then the virgin will rejoice in the dance, and the young men and the old, together, for I will turn their mourning into joy and will comfort them and give them* **joy** *for their sorrow.* Jeremiah 31:13 NASB

## L'chaim

"The four usages of the verb *śûś* in the Mosaic writings occur in Deut 28:63 and 30:9, twice in each verse. Here, amid the Mosaic warnings of the blessings and cursings, three times the Lord is pictured as one rejoicing over Israel to bless them for obedience to his Law, and once as rejoicing over them to destroy them for disobedience!"[21]

Better read that again. Rejoicing (experiencing joy) is associated with both blessings and judgment. YHVH rejoices over blessing those who are obedient. He does not withhold any good thing. He delights in granting favor. He desires to protect and provide. His actions are filled with goodness toward those who take up His instructions and adopt His way of life. But, according to the passage in Deuteronomy, He also is *glad* to punish disobedience. That seems entirely counterintuitive. We would have thought God would be sorrowful when He was forced to engage in judgment. Not so! The reason judgment is also a joyful experience

---

[21] Cohen, G. G. (1999). 2246 שׂושׂ. In R. L. Harris, G. L. Archer, Jr. & B. K. Waltke (Eds.), *Theological Wordbook of the Old Testament* (R. L. Harris, G. L. Archer, Jr. & B. K. Waltke, Ed.) (electronic ed.) (873). Chicago: Moody Press.

is that it has corrective purposes. Judgment is not wrath. It is not vengeance. It is correction. YHVH can feel joy over judgment because it is designed to *return* the wanderer to the right path. A child corrected is a delight to his parents. Just so, YHVH is delighted to act with judgment because He knows this will alter the choice of disobedience and return the prodigal to the father's home.

"*śûś* here thus seems to convey the idea of God's enthusiasm to bless the righteous and to punish the wicked. Fortunately, by God's mercy, Deut 30:9 shows that when Israel at last turns back to him, that 'the Lord will again rejoice over thee for good.'"[22]

Have you been judged—and found wanting? I have. I am keenly aware of my failures, my deliberate choices to circumvent the *mitzvot*. YHVH has *graciously* judged me. He has punished with the purpose of causing me to return to Him. He rejoices in His act because He knows it will get my attention and alter my direction. I find *joy* in His punishment when I realize that it is not retaliation but rather the loving correction of a Father who cannot countenance the thought of my absence. The husks I had to eat in the pigpen were designed to bring me to my senses—and set me on a path to return home.

Joy is my experience of blessing, and sometimes the blessing comes with bitter flavors. Joy is my ability to see that YHVH never gives up on me, never desires that I should be cast into outer darkness, never stops correcting so that I might experience the

---

[22] Ibid.

other side of joy—His cornucopia of abundance.

*Laurita writes:*

*Disaster is where sin yanked the feast off my table by grabbing the tablecloth. Curses, as delineated in Deut. 28 and other places, are a consequence of relationship fracture, of sin. The curses show up to show me the fracture points, so that I can make a correction. The curses are not punishments; no, those are reserved for the Great White Throne Judgment. The curses reflect the mercy of G-d. They give me time to repent and restore. They do NOT reflect, even in a tiny iota, what was actually incurred as a debt to Him, as well as the rest of the universe I ended up fractured from, when that fracture occurred. Putting self first messes up a whole lot more than just me! Now, how am I supposed to get all that set back right by just a little suffering?! It does not help that the sin of others messes me up, too. I can incur the curses that are the result of another's sin; in fact, sin is NEVER a solitary problem, for all sin reflects a break in relationship in some dimension, either between myself and G-d, myself and myself (yes, I can sin against myself!) or myself and others. No mere punishment can set that right. The only thing that could possibly set a break of relationship right is going to be the restoration of that relationship. (A side note of interest to me is that, in the Hebrew economy, sin against another was not considered a crime against the state(!), but instead, something that required a recompense – with interest, mind you – by the perpetrator directly back to the victim. Hmm. But I digress.)*

*I raised a pack of kids, and I was one (or is that a continuing progressive state? LOL!) too, and I can assure anyone that what a child fears most is being shut out of interaction with his or her parents. A child is viscerally connected to the parents with an emotional and spiritual umbilical cord that is not supposed to be severed until the age of puberty (bar mitzvah (or bat mitzvah)), where I hear the father is supposed to get down on his knees in front of his child and thank YHVH that he is no longer responsible for that child's direct relationship with Him! Now, a child literally becomes paralyzed; his or her growth stunts or can become completely shut down, even, if he or she gets shunted outside an active participation in the lives of the parents. Children live vicariously through the lives of their parents: they rejoice, mourn, revel in glory, or suffer as the parents do. They also learn with them. An insecure child – one that is not being adequately assured of connection – is going to be a child who is going to either be checking constantly to see if the parent is paying attention to him or her, or is going to be actively trying to get their attention, or, failing that, is going to be at least attempting, with all their might, to share their resultant misery of that lack of connection! Because a child was hardwired and designed to derive his or her very life from parents, the child cannot choose to initiate fracture, or, sin, against his or her parents. If there are relationship challenges, they will, therefore, always, as far as I have been able to tell, anyway, be at least the INITIATING fault of the parents.*

*In the lists of the types of abuse that people can suffer from, I have seen various ascending orders of severity. Starting with physical abuse (the least severe, at least in terms of long-term overall damage, surprisingly), and ranking up through verbal, emotional and sexual abuse, the lists always conclude with abandonment. Abandonment is the thing no child can adjust to. In fact, I think a child will always act out, either around others (at least to the extent he or she still feels that others can be trusted), or, if they no longer trust that their parents or others can or will connect with them, they will turn to acting out against themselves. These are the silent ones. They have decided that the only way to 'punish' the abandonment of others is to remove themselves from those others. These children have turned the rage inward. They have lost the ability to trust themselves to fix the problem. Without an exception, if asked (and when asked) these children will tell you that they would much rather have been beaten, or at least yelled at, or, or... Need I continue? Question: when does an acting-out child (a child who is suffering from incorrect relationship, or relationship fracture) get happy? When he or she gets attention! Any kind! Even the worst kind! Why? Because then they know that they haven't been abandoned: that there is still hope for them.*

*We have a Father Who delights in showing us, no matter where we are; either in relationship (blessings) or outside of it (curses) that He is never going to leave us or forsake us, no matter what we may think about it. Disaster is one way to bring relationship to a head: ask anyone who has hit bottom! Of course, there are other ways, but those other ways require at least some reciprocity on our part. Our choice, as always.*

**18.** *The Lord has rewarded me according to **my*** ***righteousness***; *according to the cleanness of my hands He has recompensed me.* Psalm 18:20 NASB

## There's Hope for Me

Want joy? Be obedient! Ah, sounds so easy, doesn't it? But that's not usually the way it works. The *yetzer ha'ra* has deep hooks in us and often manipulates us like puppets. We see the goal but we can't seem to attain it. And then, of course, we have one thousand years or more of church theology telling us that we were *born* sinful and there really isn't any hope for us apart from some supernatural act of God. We fight for a while; perhaps we progress. Then the *yetzer ha'ra*, feeling the pain of withdrawal, reasserts its power and we fall, convinced that we could never have made it in the first place. Might as well give up and just settle for the best that we can. Righteousness is a divine attribute. It can't be found in the lives of ordinary men and women like you and me.

But then there's David. Now, I wouldn't consider David a model of righteousness. In fact, we probably know more about David's sins than we do about his military and political victories. Adultery, depraved indifference, conspiring to commit murder, political corruption, deliberate disobedience to divine command—yes, David is *not* a man of great moral character and certainly not a model of righteousness. But look what he says:

"The Lord has rewarded me according to *my righteousness*." In Hebrew, *tsidqi*. The righteousness that belongs to me. My conformity to the ethical standard of YHVH. My actions along the straight path. My efforts to follow in His way. If David can say this, then I have hope. If David can say this, then so can I.

This is what we need. First, we need to know that no matter how *we* feel about our sins, God feels grace toward us. Second, we need to recognize that gratitude is an important first step toward changing our ways, but it isn't enough to keep us going. Third, we need to realize that *our best interests* are served by conforming our lives to what delights Him. Fourth, we must affirm that what really drives our behavior is not our thinking but rather our feelings, and that this is not a bad thing. What we *do* with these emotions is the critical issue. Fifth, we must come to terms with the fact that we have trained ourselves to operate according to the solutions presented by the *yetzer ha'ra* for a very long time. Sixth, we must abandon these habitual patterns even though we will often not see any other route to take care of our emotional needs. But the only way we can have hope of doing this is to know that our efforts *can succeed*. And so, finally, we must trust that our righteousness, our efforts to conform our lives to His instructions, *really do matter*. They make a difference that YHVH honors. They change our world. And God will reward us for those efforts. Yes, He will continue to judge us in order to bring us into full alignment, but that only means that judgment is a form of blessing intended to lead us into even greater blessing.

With all this in mind, we are called upon to *act*. We are equipped to feel the pain and sorrow that will lead us to the experience of hope and joy. We can use all these powerful and crafted emotions to bring us into His presence; and that is what we really want. Day 18.

*Laurita writes:*

*Oh, how I love step-by-step, blow-by-blow instructions! Whoo hoo! Excellent walk-out description. If salvation is precipitated by my repentance, sanctification (that neglected "S" word!) is a process that I participate in by virtue of my willingness. We want G-d to be willing to save us. He is. But then, we have to be willing to let Him gradually pull us all the way out of our mud. That's the sanctification part. We get to worrying about 'losing our salvation'; well, He isn't going anywhere! I think we are the ones who keep insisting that salvation is not where we really wanted to be. We are trained to think that, because we are defective, salvation is not possible RIGHT NOW, so it must be something that happens after life in the here-and-now, but, if you actually go looking in that whole Book, nowhere does it say that salvation happens later. Instead, it tells me that NOW is the day of repentance; NOW is the day of salvation; IF we do not do what? Harden our hearts to the sanctification process that salvation is the ticket TO. We are the ones who keep trying to throw ourselves back over the fence. It's not Him; it's me who can't make up my mind if I really like to be free or not!*

106

*Chains are the things that attract and bind the yetzer ha-ra. Because I am used to them; they FEEL like security, even though what they are really securing me in is my own death. Agreement with hell is an agreement to NOT LIVE in this particular moment. Agreement with hell is hedge betting on the certainty that my yetzer ha-ra operates out of – the certainty that I am not going to make it out of here alive. The freedom and trust that the grace of salvation keeps trying to hand me instead, are the scary things that keep throwing me back over the edge of my destruction and stupor, into love and life, but they feel like freefall without a bungee cord! Not safe at all! Death is what is certain (well, in my world, there's also taxes!): life is that unknown variable. Life is the thing I DO NOT KNOW up front. Life is, in fact, the thing I cannot know until it happens. Why? Why can't I 'control' (predetermine) reality? I think that's the wrong question. I think the question should be why do I want to? Well, I think I suffer from the illusion that I should be able to control my life because there is a part of me that remembers the Garden experience where every part of existence was slammed into full gear, and the pedal of my personal righteousness – which is the full power of being IN the love that righteousness affords me – was jammed on the floor, and all my lights were green. I remember that there was such a thing as nothing in opposition to me (hey, because I would not be operating in opposition to it, of course. Details!). Control, it turns out, is an extremely poor substitute for what we really long for, which is a totally frictionless, seamless, full-tilt-boogie into the future. Actually managing to be able to lose myself in love, which is what righteousness returns me to, is a thrill; a rush*

107

*that no sin has ever been able to duplicate (even though we do keep trying!). 'Controlling' my own life turns out to be a very poor substitute for the experience of having love control me. 'Controlling' life, on closer examination, turns out to actually be all about hedge-betting on my own death, which is the only certainty that the yetzer ha-ra really knows, and that is because my flesh knows nothing about eternity; but love is all about eternity.*

*Could we talk about eternity? C.S. Lewis's book, The Great Divorce, really challenged me, because in it he proposed that heaven and hell are realities that can both backdate and postdate the past and the future. The gradual accumulation of the sum total of my choices can determine, in retrospect, what my whole life was – and is going to be – about. Now, if time is a linear river, that makes no sense. Up until right now, my whole life has just been sucky and that's that. Nothing in the present and future can possibly change that part. BUT, salvation is the thing that returns me to some aspects of participation in the righteousness, the rightly-relating, of Yeshua, and that is a perfection of relationship that is outside of time. If I ultimately choose destruction, my past is going to prove to be an inevitable downward spiral of relationship fracture toward that end, but when I choose life, that choice does something curious with my past. Hosea records the promise that the years the locusts ate can be restored to us. What?! But, in my experience so far, I think I have seen how that could be so. The anguish of my heart, all those sucky years, had to do with breaks of relationship. It had nothing to do with the fortunes and vicissitudes of life. The flesh focuses on the temporal; the heart is about the spiritual, and the spirit knows no time or place. There is a space outside of time where the deepest longings of my heart can be fulfilled, and in that place, eternity operates in full power. Love really can make all things possible. Eternity is something that I can plug into right now! Can G-d heal the fractures of my past? Yes! This is a marvelous part of the salvation package, and, to me, anyway, is one of its better perks. I have been finding that the best thing I have ever done for all the people in my life that I have loved and despaired about is to get myself saved! From that position, then, G-d can rework all the disasters of my life – all the heartbreaks, into something new. And, He has been! Hallelujah! Love is amazing stuff, folks.*

**19.** *Whoever gives thought to **the way** he lives in this world will merit divine salvation.* Tractate Moed Katan page 5 folio a

## *Feeling True*

You and I have every reason to examine how we live. In fact, this examination is our only hope of actually changing direction and meriting God's favor. Of course, as you must know by now, this has nothing to do with the way YHVH feels about us. His everlasting *hen* is as much a part of who He is as His holiness. But it has everything to do with us. We must act in accordance with what we are commanded to do and what we are able to do; and that means separating the wheat from the chaff. In the words of the Sages, giving thought to the way we live now.

Over the last few weeks we have been giving thought to the way we live. Hopefully you have discovered something about your feelings regarding life, the assumptions you've made about living and the consequences you have borne as a result. Hopefully some of this examination has caused you to shift a bit, to change your course, to remove what doesn't belong and take on those things that matter most. Hopefully you have discovered a way to trust Him more, and put less of yourself in the ethical equation.

But sometimes even all this isn't quite enough. Sometimes we know perfectly well what must be left behind, what must be embraced, how we must trust more to His care—and we are still *emotionally unable*. Sometimes we have been crippled by the past so deeply that we limp the rest of our lives. Jacob discovered that his ability to manipulate things in his favor ran up against the wall of the will of God. For the rest of his life, he limped. Perhaps you have also encountered that stranger in the night, the one who will not be defeated and who causes you some permanent telltale sign of your struggle. What then? What's left after limping?

Jacob's injury became a permanent reminder of his vulnerability. That's what's left. We must have some reminder that we are vulnerable – that we are still broken – that we can't walk without help. I suspect, as my friend John once said to me, that you and I have pushed the intellectual aspect of this exploration to its utter limit. On this side of the brook Kidron, we have come face to face with the inadequacies of our attempts to find a *rational* solution, a *controlled* outcome. We have reached the end of the mental analysis – and have been defeated. What is left is crossing the brook and entering into a new form of life, a new way to engage the world. What is left is *experience*, not more analysis. We must *experience* the care of the Lord if we are going to survive. We must *feel* His compassion, not because the verses tell us He is compassionate but because someone wipes away our tears. Someone holds us in the night.

There is no more *thinking*. The *yetzer ha'ra* has full command of that avenue. There is only the raw emotion of who we are, where we have been, what we have become—and the desperate desire to cross this brook without dying. I *know* that God cares. Now I need to feel His care. I feel afraid. I fear being alone. I feel empty. Now I need to *feel loved* even if it hurts. The Sages tell me that if I am able to bring these feelings to the light of His countenance, if I will allow Him to examine the ways I have protected, then I will merit His grace. Then I will find deliverance. Then I will wade across.

*Laurita writes:*

*Why am I frozen? It is fear. Why do I hide? It is shame. Why cannot I receive love? Because I am carrying my guilt. Why do I want to run from where I am, or at least cover it all up with pretense or an altered state of reality? Because I cannot stand myself! Why will I get up tomorrow and do the same things I did today? Because, where my mind has not been renewed by the washing of the water of the Word, I am still insane, and the hallmark of insanity is the repetition of the same action or thoughts, with the expectation of a different result this time. Y'all, this is the closest I ever get to faith or hope in my flesh! Pitiful, isn't it?*

*I stand with Paul, who said that he did what he didn't want to do, and didn't do what he wanted to do. This is double-mindedness, which leaves me unstable in all my ways. I cannot even WANT to do right sometimes! There is nothing in my flesh that finds sin repugnant; the only thing my flesh wants is to get away with it, and the only thing my flesh is ever sorry for is getting caught. But, at the end of my day, guilt and grief overwhelm me. I mourn when it is too late. I suffer after the tent comes down and everybody goes home. When I am all alone, the tidal wave of my day hits me. And, once again, I cannot stand myself.*

*I cannot receive the love of G-d in my flesh; nor can I receive the love of myself or others. I cannot receive it because fear says I cannot trust it, guilt says I don't deserve it, and shame says, well, the only thing shame ever says: hide! I cannot give love in my flesh, either, because love seeks to give, but all my flesh has to offer is need and greed – or actions that attempt to cover that need or greed so as to serve need and greed better! To give and receive love is the fulfilling of the Law (relationship), but the flesh is utterly incapable of love. Worshiping Self as the only 'safe' source; believing lies that leave me confused and shattered, regarding all else and others as essential competition, or as downright enemies, I am isolated in what Paul calls the enmity of the flesh: I am fractured. I am going nowhere in this position! I have no power from here, because I am stuck in a place where I have no choices left except the lesser of two or more evils. I find I cannot choose my way back out of disaster, because the disaster IS the lack of the freedom to choose! But G-d! He left me exactly one choice in my flesh; one choice that no sin, except the unpardonable one, can ever separate me from, and that is the choice to stop. I can quit. I can lay down my arms. I can cry "uncle!" For decades, I believed to the bottom of my soul that I could never quit – that it was righteousness to keep on 'trying my best'. At the bottom of my Self-sourcing soul, I think, if I am to be utterly honest with myself, that I was suffering from the insane thought that the whole universe might collapse – or at least all my fears would come true – if I gave up.*

113

*Sitting in a twelve-step meeting, trying to find a way to do what the third step suggested, and find a way to turn my will and my life over to the care of G-d, I ran into the key that broke my self-imposed conundrum. Someone suggested that I stop trying to think of it as giving up, and try to think of it as giving IN. All of a sudden, the confusion cleared, and I could see. The universe might not collapse after all, if I handed it over to Him to hold! So, for just micro-seconds at a time, I started trying to do that. Baby steps toward trust.*

*If I stop the insanity of thinking it is all up to me, the fear recedes. If I stop trying to justify myself, I quit carrying my guilt around like the burden that it truly is. The advantage of confessing my sin is that at that point He can defend me; He can revenge me; He can justify me. If I humble up and face the music; if I quit trying to run (like, how far did I ever get, anyway?!), shame no longer has a legal right to torment me. Shame only exists in places where pride is still trying to keep a toe hold. Repent for pride, and shame will vanish, too! It's a two-for-one deal! To get rid of the bad stuff, I have to become willing to trade it in for the good stuff. In the kingdom of Self, where every mistake is fatal(!), fear, guilt, and shame are my cruel taskmasters. I have to choose to accept the rule of a new Master before I can get out from under the old ones, but this new Master says He is my yoke Buddy: if I agree to go the Way He is going, He will pull my load: my accumulation of fracture and its resulting baggage, if I agree to pull His load in return. Y'all, He isn't dragging anything! That's light enough! All I have to lose in this deal is my dross. What a trade! Hallelujah!*

**20.** *Where there is **no vision**, the people are unrestrained, but happy is he who keeps the law.* Proverbs 29:18 NASB

## *A Step in the Right Direction*

Maybe, not yet. Maybe we aren't quite ready for total abandonment to the directions of the Lord. Maybe we're scared that if we actually let go of everything we have used to prop us up during those emotional rollercoaster rides, we will fall—hard! More than fall. Die! Emotionally. Yes, we have all the promises—in words—but maybe that isn't quite enough. After all, words are not feelings. Words are part of the cyber-cognitive rationalization world that refused to provide the touchy-feely relief that we needed from "words." Words can be a tool of the enemy, convincing us that we can somehow manage in a world controlled by thought. Words betrayed us. They said, "We will tell you the secret," but instead they led us into a dark corner where we found ourselves imprisoned by our own rationalizations. Words gave us doctrine. We needed kisses.

Oswald Chambers writes, "When once we lose sight of God, we begin to be reckless, we cast off certain restraints, we cast off praying, we cast off the vision of God in little things, and begin to act on our own initiative. If we are eating what we have out of our own hand, doing things on our own initiative without expecting God to come in, we are on the downward path, we have lost the vision."[23]

---

[23] Oswald Chambers, *My Utmost for His Highest*, May 9.

Some translations of this verse would have us believe that "vision" is about prophecy. The Hebrew *hazon* certainly contains that possibility. With this in mind, we assume that what is missing is the voice of the prophet or the clear understanding of the prophetic word. We are back to cognitive transmission. But *hazon* is more than a description of the "seer" or his message. *Hazon* is used to describe virtually *any form of received sensation or perception.* I'm guessing that the author didn't have email or sermons or even "a word of prophecy" in mind. Chambers is much closer to the truth. When we fail to *feel the awe of YHVH,* we are no longer compelled to live before Him. Heschel suggests that the first step is awe. The first sensory awareness is majesty. The first impact on my oh-so-self-involved fearful and shame-bound life is to be struck down by His glory. It's not words that will save me. It's His presence!

Maybe we aren't quite ready to jump off the cliff of reckless trust because we lack the sensory impact of *who He is.* Maybe we are like Peter who suggested altars on the mountaintop rather than dirt in his face. Yes, we need those promises, but they are just more words in the battle with the words of the *yetzer ha'ra.* And the *yetzer ha'ra* knows we must *feel.* What we need in order to let go of all those tiny little indiscretions that keep us sane are kisses.

"Lord, oh Lord. If I take a step toward You, will You still run to meet me with a kiss?" Day 20.

*Laurita writes:*

*What the world needs is love. We are afraid of all our needs. I would not need love if I had it. I am afraid because I do NOT have it. "Kiss the Son, lest he be angry, and ye perish from the way..." (Ps. 2:12") "Let him kiss me with the kisses of his mouth: for thy love (is) better than wine..." (Prov. 1:2) I need to be touched: I need the touch that electrifies; wounds; paralyzes and heals: the touch that makes me forget what I was going to say, or think. 'Teched', in hill parlance, where I came from, referred to being just a little crazy; a teched person did not quite have it all together; they didn't know who they were any more. We all want the transmission scrambled; we all want to be touched; we all want to start over.*

*Ok, this is going to date me. Remember when we thought the newest, best idea was to develop a way to completely 'bliss out'; a way that removed all distracting sensory perception? We thought that if we could only achieve that, we would perhaps have found the shortcut to nirvana. So the sensory deprivation tanks were conceived. I remember how people were so excited: they were lining up for the chance to experience what was proving so hard, by regular means – like chanting or meditating, say – to reach 'oneness'; to get to peace. So we all held our breaths while the first people hung in tanks of lukewarm water, with no sight or sound or anything to TOUCH to distract them from peace. And what did we find? That we had actually found a way to drive ourselves crazy in very short order. Sensory deprivation, in fact, is torture of the first magnitude. NO one was able to last in those tanks. They came flying out of there and said "don't ever do that to me again!" I remember the disappointment. It was*

119

*a big shock and a letdown. So much for peace the 'nothingness' route!*

*So we looked for peace by flooding all our receptor sites with drugs and experiential practices that sent us in overdrive; that pushed our sensory perception to the point that we could believe we 'connected' to everything and everybody. Shortcuts to righteousness. So, were we REALLY connected? Did we achieve world peace with our music-a-thons and rallies: did we really get all the way up that stairway to heaven: was Lucy really in the sky with diamonds?*

*What keeps me from His Presence? What keeps me from my Lover? What insulates me from the electrical connection with reality and its Source? He created an entire universe designed to overwhelm me with awe; gave me five senses and then surrounded me with an unending stream of ways to tell me that He is love, and that He loves me, so why cannot I FEEL that?*

*I find I don't need His Presence as the thing I EARN; as my reward for being good; I need His Presence to be able to move at all! I am lost; lost in trespasses and sins; frozen in my iniquity and the iniquity of those who trespassed against me, all of which destroyed my ability to trust. In fact, what I suffer from is a profound lack of trust, and to the extent I cannot trust, I have no spiritual connection; no way to EXPERIENCE love. What I need most, I am fractured from. Oh, who shall deliver me from this body of death – this torturous inability to feel – this inability to reach out and touch?*

*I need deliverance. I need Someone to get me out of the tank RIGHT NOW. I need deliverance from every rock I shoved my need for love under – every practice of death that I use to insulate me from the intolerable fracture of the trust I need – the faith I must have to take even as much as one step into the arms of love. Where there is no experience of trust in my life, I am perishing. The biggest sin in my life – the biggest fracture that keeps me from connection, from relationship, from the sensory experience of love, is the surfeit of faith. One of the most useful prayers for me to emulate is that of the father who cried "help thou my unbelief". Fear is what shows up when I break trust. To get trust back, I must be delivered from my fear.*

*Fear, in fact, is a sin that must be repented of, but that is good news. There is all the difference in the world between choosing to face fear and wade back through it to find the cause for it, and choosing all the practices of death the world offers to shove that fear under rocks. Fear is not the thing I have to endure: fear is what I can repent for as soon as it shows its slimy face! Fear is the closest the yetzer ha-ra comes to the experience of awe, but it is a poor substitute! No wonder we get them confused! Fear floods the receptor sites that were designed to receive love. Trust is what opens the door to love. When I face my fears, I find that they are all caused by putting my faith in things that are not true. When I repent for fear, I re-open my heart to believe the Truth instead. It is fear that keeps me from the awe I experience in the Presence of that Truth.*

**21.** *Where there is no vision, the people are* **unrestrained**, *but happy is he who keeps the law.* Proverbs 29:18 NASB

## *My Freedom*

"Why can't you just leave me alone?" Of course, that doesn't mean I want *no one* around (well, sometimes I really don't want to have anyone around). What I mean is that I don't want *your interference.* I want my version of freedom. In Hebrew this is called *para.* It's an interesting word. In one form it means, "to act as leader, to lead." In another form it means, "to let go, to cut loose, to act without restraint." That makes sense. Everyone knows that the leader does what he wants. In fact, if I add a final *aleph* to this word, I get another word that expresses my desire to do what I want without question—*pharaoh.* The one who lives an *unrestrained* life. The little god.

When we no longer see (experience) the awe and majesty of the one true God, YHVH, we live like little pharaohs. We become our own gods. We cut loose from delighting Him. We no longer act according to our apprehension of His power and might. As Oswald says, "We cast off" all kinds of practices and provisions that belong to the Kingdom of heaven while we create a kingdom on earth—and discover, only too late, that we are enslaved to our own desires. My version of freedom is bondage to myself. No army in the world can overcome that force of habit. I don't fail in my efforts to reform and become a "good" person because I lack some prophetic word. I have all the words that I could ever need, collected in a nice leather bound book on my shelf. I fail because I no longer experience the awe of YHVH in my daily existence. Without a sense of *majesty*, my world collapses into the little kingdom of pharaoh, and I spend my day taking care of my own needs.

When Heschel says that a man's vision must exceed his grasp, he does not mean that we need to set goals for bigger houses, faster cars and yachts. He means our view of life must include *what is beyond this life*. It must include the vision of God's purposes, experienced as a present reality in my choices today. Without this perspective *and experience*, I will have little motivation to deny those pressing emotional needs in order to serve a greater good. I will let go of the heavenly bonds in order to have earthly freedom. I will enter the prison because its walls protect me.

Solomon's wisdom informs me that happiness is found in *keeping* Torah. Happiness is not the product of unrestrained living. Pharaoh (and all like him) was not happy. He was "free" to be enslaved to his own ego, but that is a far cry from "happy." This verse uses the Hebrew *'eser*, "blessed, happy" as the proper description for someone who has discovered that Torah living means walking in the wide open spaces where God and Man commune in peace. We prodigals take steps toward the rushing approach of YHVH when we decide today to be happy in the commandments. Pick one. Do it. Feel the wonder. Day 21.

*Laurita writes:*

*Free to be me. Free to love. I must be free before I can worship Him. To move in 360 degrees – to have all my choices returned to me – IS freedom: is power, love and a sound mind. In the Middle East there is a Sufi sect of Mohammedanism called the Whirling Dervishes, who are devoted to ecstatic meditation which includes whirling. The act of whirling, as far as I can tell, is an attempt to leave the ego behind and create the experience of love, which is freedom of movement equally in all directions. (It looks like really hard work to me!)*

*Evil, as seen through the looking glass, is an attempt to create love in the flesh. Evil is not about hate: evil is not about fear: evil is about lying. In fact, evil would be telling the truth if it told us that it was about those things. No, all evil lies to us and we fall for the lie because it holds out the illusion that we can recreate love on our own: we can have all the accouterments and advantages and attributes, even, of love, but we can leave the Lover behind, and create another one to take His place. So we extend the right hand of fellowship – which is the hand that should have been exclusively His – to devils. We would have been better off if we had cut it off, y'all!*

*"Without a sense of majesty, my world collapses into the little kingdom of pharaoh, and I spend my day taking care of my own needs." This sentence sums up perfectly why the world is suffering! What have we lost? First and foremost, we have lost that sense of majesty, which is the experience of purpose, and which is also the place I must be in before my*

*ego is able to relax. (I think of the ego as a little hyper-alert system that gauges whether or not I am correctly experiencing love – a most necessary little instrument, and one that is much abused and maligned, I would have to say!) We were created in the image of G-d, which is to say we are to be an expression of purpose – a determiner of reality – a channel of super-connection that ties the rest of it together. This is why the rest of creation as we know it looks to us to be a steward to it. A steward gives purpose; determines meaning, if you will, to what he or she is serving. We are the crowning act of creation because we are to provide majesty: when we show up on the scene, we are to be the embodiment of the Majesty of heaven to the rest of creation. We are to serve, or be able to provide function – and therefore meaning – to it. All creation waits to do our bidding. Our choices must therefore remain free – remain POSSIBLE – in all directions. Why? I think it is because at any moment, at any point, the Lord of the dance may step literally ANYWHERE, and we need to be able to keep up!*

*So if I am not supposed to serve my own needs: if I was created to serve the needs of all the rest of creation instead, then how are mine going to be met? Here lies the true beauty of the system. What do I need? ALL of my needs are rooted in the need to love and be loved. In the act of continually reaching out to the Source of love for the purposes of obtaining the love necessary to carry out the injunction to be that steward (this is the essence of the dance), I am freeing up a flow of love that is tremendous enough to satisfy all the rest of creation. When I am lined up correctly in obedience of Torah,*

126

*I have placed myself in the right place for that Love to pour through me on its Way to everything and everyone else. This is the purpose for which I have been made in the image of that Source: I was made to be a little, or, derivative, source for all else. When you look at it like that, it is like asking whether I would choose to be the beginning and the end for just me, or whether I want to be that for everything and everyone else. The differential is staggering. No wonder our egos are suffering! They are screaming out for that huge flow: that non-ending stream of Love that is necessary before we are fulfilling our true function. Serving my own needs? That is a joke! What we really desire is to manage the World Bank! No wonder the ego is insatiable! Perhaps we would do well to start listening to what our egos really have to say.*

**22.** *Many* are saying of me, *"God will not deliver him."* But you, Lord, are a shield around me, Psalm 3:2-3a NIV

## Who Says?

"Many are saying." But who? Whose voices are telling us that God will not deliver us? If I listen very carefully, I know those voices. I have heard them before – many times. It is the chorus of my inner choir, the sounds of the *yetzer ha'ra*. **I** am the one saying to myself, "God will not deliver me." Of course, I know (cognitively) that He *could* if He chose to, but I feel no more precious than the pigs in the pen. Why would He rescue me from a prison that I myself have constructed to keep Him out?

Certainly David must have felt just like this on those nights he could not sleep because his guilt removed him from the presence of the Holy One of Israel. He cried out. He wept. He agonized. But the voice of the Lord could not overpower the voices of David's own *epithumia*, his desire for Bathsheba, his desire to uphold a reputation he already knew he had lost, his desire to pretend that things were still normal in his house. Ambushed by passion, he must have wondered if the Lord of hosts would ever open His arms to have him back. Bathsheba was still there. Uriah's grave was still there. The crown was still there. But peace in David's world was gone—and there seemed no way to recover it. He could not go back and undo the conspiracy. Better to just pretend—and wrestle in his nightmares.

Then something happened. A man came who threw open the door, exposed the shame, revealed the treachery and the sin. David was broken. The pretense was over. Confession, repentance, punishment, atonement, restitution. There is no other way. If we could only have the courage to admit we are powerless in the face of those threats to our emotional well-being. If we could only admit that we deliberately turned to our own devices just to stop hurting. If we could just say, "Yes, that's me" and give ourselves permission to feel our desperation. Then we might be able to say with David, "But you, Lord, are a shield around me."

"Our *yetzer ha'ra* is part and parcel of our very constitution. It is the record of every disappointment, rejection, and failure that reaches us from beyond our self-enclosure, from the lives of others who have had a share in bringing us into being. This accumulation of pain is justifiably called the *yetzer ha'ra*, which pushes us to obscure the view of the other in our souls through the diversions of everyday life."[24]

What does this mean? It means that *healing will hurt!* There is no anesthetic for the pain of confession. We have been taking "pills" of one form or another for years in order not to feel this pain, but the only cure is to stop medicating and let it come. In fact, as long as we pursue *anything* that prevents us from feeling this accumulation of pain, we cannot get well. Day 22.

---

[24] Ira Stone's commentary in Moses Luzzatto's *Mesillat Yesharim*, p. 39.

*Laurita writes:*

*I used to catch myself running from the disasters of my life, and I used that observation to beat myself up. There is this terrible little fact I learned about the yetzer ha-ra, and it is that, in my flesh, I have no forgiveness to offer myself or others, but neither can I accept to forgiveness of myself, G-d or others. This is because in my flesh I react to everything I perceive as an impediment to Getting What I Want – and that would include the choices and actions of fracture from reality (sin) of myself as well as others – as a disaster of the first order, and the only way my flesh can see to correct such behavior is to condemn it – to outlaw it – to sentence it severely so as to 'make' it not want to EVER do that again to me! In other words, I guilt-trip it. Guilt is the natural reaction of the flesh to sin. I think guilt is a curse, in fact. I do it to myself, as well as others, but I think it is also a sin in and of itself. Why? Because I think guilt is even further rebellion and I think that that is because my guilt, like all other sin, has the effect of driving me even further away; of setting me up to do even yet more sin. I think this is because guilt is evidence of my fracture – is condemnation of that fracture, in fact – and my flesh has no natural defense against condemnation of any kind. All I can do in the natural with that condemnation is to either justify myself (excuses), blame (judge and condemn myself, others or G-d) or, failing all that: RUN! HIDE! Destroy evidence! Change the Law! (Well, I could continue, but, sadly, we all know that list, I think!) In fact, I have been delivered over to the tormentors, and they are going to beat me until I*

131

*come up with every last penny that I owe, which I can never do because my flesh stays broke. I have met the enemy, and it is certainly me! I think we run from our guilt, like we run from all the other evidence of our fracture, because we can do nothing about it, and none of us can stand that failure. Guilt is the fuel, in fact, in my get-away car. I can run on guilt! Many of us do! We get up in the morning (don't we), and remind ourselves of ALL the things we know we have done wrong; we beat ourselves up about them so we won't want to EVER do them again; and then, while we are standing at that pump, we naturally fill up the tank for the whole day! I used to run all day on guilt. Guilt motivated me to toe the line – to make sure I NEVER made a mistake: guilt was my unholy spirit, and the closest thing to a conscience I could afford. I used guilt, in fact, as the false conscience for my little kingdom of the flesh, because the flesh cannot abide the voice of G-d.*

*When I was small, my mama used to read Pilgrim's Progress to us, and I used to think the most mysterious thing in that whole story was the burden that Pilgrim carried on his back. I wondered why it was there: why and how it got there, why he had to carry it, why he couldn't get it back off, and what tied it on. I resolved, in my little flesh, that that was stupid (I judged him!) and concluded that I was not going to go around with a pack on my back. That way, I would never have to stand in front of that horrible cross. I resolved, in fact, to be 'perfect'. No guilt for me! Well! (No comment. LOL!)*

*Guilt has the legal right to torment me as long as I am in rebellion – it is, in fact, evidence of the first order that I am IN rebellion. Unless and until I surrender, guilt is a blessing (perceived in my flesh as a curse!) that gives me motivation to repent; it gives me time to lay down my arms so that I am not instantly consumed; time to yelp for help, in fact, like all the other curses, but guilt does not give me a WAY to do that. To undo the spell of sin; to "work it backwards with dissevering mutters", I have to unravel the snarl (don't you just love that word?) I have to start at the root of the problem. I think guilt was given to me in mercy, as all the curses were, to be a guide out of my hole in that other kingdom, and, like the other curses, can buy me the time I need to repent, but guilt is not from G-d (only conviction is), and guilt is certainly not my friend!*

*When I see guilt, I should start there. Guilt is the closest I get to the Temple; guilt can get me right up to the wall, in fact, but the only way I am going to actually get in the Wicker Gate is to present my invitation to the Kingdom. How do I get such a precious thing? Guilt condemns me, but it also gives me the right next-order of operations, if I will take it. Guilt drives me to my knees with the intolerable load of my sense of fracture, but if I do not choose to take that next step, I am still sinning: I am still in rebellion. No, while I am on those knees, in the correct posture as a supplicant – in fact, in the place where I have nothing left to lose, where I have no more impediments to keep me from repentance – I must actually repent for that rebellion. I must surrender; I must lay down my arms, and request entrance in through that Gate to that other Kingdom. However, I do not get to keep guilt in that Kingdom as my little secret – private unholy spirit. No, I have to hand guilt over, along*

133

*with all the other tools that I have been using to ply my Self trade – all that other unholy spiritual fuel in my tank, such as the spirits of bitterness, shame, jealousy, unloving, rejection, and fear, et al. No, in this Kingdom, there is only One Spirit, and I do not use Him; He uses me. I have to repent for using guilt as a substitute for refusing to heed the voice of G-d, which is the gentle conviction of conscience that is the voice of the Holy Spirit in my soul. In fact, I think guilt is what my flesh uses as its substitute for the voice of G-d (conscience), and as such, the use of guilt is a sin to be repented of.*

*Guilt, like bitterness (unforgiveness), actually is a killer of the first magnitude. Guilt is one of those "dead works" (works that are going to kill me) that I think Paul keeps referring to. Guilt, in fact, is what I use to cement myself in my rebellion, but the curse of that guilt will drive me to my destruction, and it will destroy me every step of that way. Guilt will weigh me down: it will literally knot my muscles and disfigure my joints and coagulate the platelets in my blood. Guilt can cause depression and rage, and in my case, probable schizophrenia. Guilt manifests itself in our lives in many ways. Again, I would like to invite anybody who wishes to consider guilt in the context of the whole nephesh experience, to try to find on YouTube the thoughtful and prayerful work done on this subject by Dr. Frans J. Cronje of South Africa, who has been faithfully seeking to know and to apply the excellent direction we have been given in Scripture – particularly in Deuteronomy 28. It is time we turn around and face our guilt. We have been given everything we need to do so, and there is no other place we can go. My guilt is why that Cross was raised. Hallelujah!*

**23.** *But you, Lord, are a **shield** around me, my glory, the One who lifts my head high. I call out to the Lord, and he answers me from his holy mountain.* Psalm 3:3-4 NIV

## In the Garden

We know what a shield is, right? It's a piece of armor designed to protect the one who bears it. We have plenty of historical examples. Ah, but our history, the history of Western warfare, diverts us from David's meaning. We should have realized that there was something odd about this "shield" when he says that it *surrounds* him. Our images of shield don't do that. In fact, the word David uses is *magen*, derived from the Hebrew *ganan* ("to defend') and also the root of *gan* or *ganna* ("garden"). What David has in mind is not a piece of metal that I hold in front of me but rather a wall or hedge that surrounds me. In other words, a protected *garden*.

*Gan Eden*, the Garden of Eden, is such a place. When I enjoy the presence of the Lord, I am in *gan Eden*, his protected garden. I am surrounded by everything that He put behind the secure wall, everything that delights Him. I am free to roam this garden knowing that all He placed in it is purposeful and beneficial. Even the Tree. I have no fear in the garden because it belongs to the Creator God and He oversees it. I have a job to do in this garden – to care for it, to husband it, to steward it – but I am not the creator of this place of protection. He is. His *magen*, His *ganna*, encloses me.

When YHVH surrounds me with His protective hedgerow, He is my glory. "Glory" is the word *kavad*. It is a word often used in its metaphorical sense of significant, important or worthy. David proclaims that in the safety of God's garden he knows that YHVH gives him significance. David's importance is the *extension* of the majesty of YHVH. The very fact that YHVH has placed him within the protected garden is a sure sign that David *matters to God*.

What do we learn from David's declaration? Has the Lord protected you? Has He placed you within His garden? If you look carefully at the course of your life, do you see that He has been watching over you? Do you notice that some things that could have happened, that should have happened to you, didn't? Can you see that all that you *deserved* didn't come to pass? Why not? Was it because you were actually in the garden without realizing it? Were you actually surrounded by His protection but, like Jacob, you didn't know that God was in this place? And now that you see it, what do you think? What do you feel?

Do you realize, at last, that you are safe? ". . . to be swept by the enigma and to pause – rather that to flee and to forget – is to live within the [garden]."[25] Day 23.

*Laurita writes:*

*"...to be swept by the enigma and to pause – rather*

---

[25] Abraham Heschel, *Man Is Not Alone*, p. 16.

*than to flee and to forget – is to live within the (garden)."*

*How do I get to such a response? How do I stay there? How do I overcome the impulse to flee and forget: to run in terror and shame and to seek altered states of reality because reality cannot be faced in my own skin? How do I rest in His love? How do I stay and worship in His holy mountain, instead of either being chased back down it by my sin, or just passing out; or, worse, continue to defy Him; continue to block that love and that care because I cannot trust its Source?*

*What has to change?*

*Repentance. "Put away the sin that is among (between) you" then "I will be your God, and you shall be my people." Holiness. Set apartness. Purity from the sin that defiles. The cherubim stand at the gate to that Garden with flaming swords to keep out all who would presume to avail themselves of the Tree of Life that grows within, without purifying themselves; without purging themselves of sin first. We desire to live forever in that Garden, which is a righteous desire, but we desire to do so in our flesh which, because our flesh is unclean, pollutes that desire, and so we desire immortality for immoral purposes. Because we do not worship Him in spirit and in truth, but rather in our flesh and for deceitful, hidden purposes, our offering is not consumed with the fire of consummation, and we cannot stay.*

*If I am to be swept off my feet by love then I must become willing to "set aside the sin that so easily besets (me)" and lay down my arms in exchange for*

138

*His. Sin sets me in opposition to all that the Garden represents. It is my own rebellion that keeps me from resting – from staying in His love. "There is no peace, I say, for the wicked." The troubled sea of the world has no rest, but the Garden is all about rest. The Sabbath, then, is probably the closest we get to it this side of eternity. The Sabbath, kept correctly, gives us a WAY to stay, because, if we follow the instructions for the Sabbath correctly, we learn to follow the sequence of actions we need to take to get ourselves to true rest; or, relief from sin and its consequences (the tormentors; or, curses).*

*What are the Sabbath instructions? Let's look at Friday – or, preparation day. What do we do then? First, we wrap up the business of the flesh, then we prepare nourishment, then we conduct a mikvah, or ritual cleansing for ourselves, as well as what surrounds us: THEN, we welcome the Sabbath; or, place in time to commune with our Maker. What then has the Sabbath been given to us – as a template, or a picture? The Sabbath, by design, shows us – reminds us – of the correct order of operations to get ourselves out of the sin that drives us, enslaves us and keeps us from rest (peace) so that we can be free to worship (connect) with our Lover, Who can stand no degree of separation (sin).*

*Ok, let's go back and look again. First, I have to forsake my 'own' ambitions, desires and unholy alliances of the flesh, and submit myself back to His Will instead. As nature abhors a vacuum, I must replace the desire of the flesh (sin) with His Will, which I find in His Word. I must renew my mind with the washing of the water of the Word. That Word is the Bread of Life that I must have to live forever, and represents the Tree of Life to me right now. I must obey its instructions and stand on its promises before I have the fortitude, the nourishment that I must have to withstand evil. Last but not least, I must repent for my sins before the sun goes down on the day of my salvation. I must be clean before the sun sets, and my Lord shows up to walk in the cool of that evening with me again and talk to me face to face. If I am not free of sin; if I am not clean; then I am going to run and hide from that Face and cry for the rocks to fall on me.*

*My sins of rebellion separate me; they fracture and isolate me from Him. If I am to stand there in my own skin, then that skin had better be clean! This is what the Sabbath teaches me, but it gives me more than that! The Sabbath gives me the venue for worship here and now. If I follow the instructions, I have a way and a place (time) to commune with Him, which I must have to live. In my sin, I can't live with Him; I cannot worship; I cannot be "swept by the enigma, and pause", for my sin will not allow me the freedom of awe. It is humility that allows me the experience of awe, but the shame of my sin keeps me from that humility. To repent and forsake sin then, is to free me so that I can return to my true natural state. Repentance, by means of that altar before the Gate, is what allows me entrance back into that Garden, which only the truly humble will enter. Only repentance can free me from shame (that keeps me in hiding) and returns me to the freedom I need to obey, but obedience is only possible from a truly humble heart. It is the humility that comes from true obeisance (now THERE'S a word we should not have left behind!) that allows me into that Presence, which is the Source of all awe. Worship is only possible with "clean hands and a pure heart". Awe is something a wicked heart can never truly know, then, but awe in that Presence is also what the Garden is all about.*

**24.** *But you, Lord, are a shield around me, my glory, the One who lifts my head high. I call out to the Lord, and **he answers** me from his holy mountain.* Psalm 3:3-4 NIV

## *I Am Not Alone*

You know there's just a possibility that all this time we just weren't listening. David cries out. God answers. Do you suppose God decided *not* to answer when we cried out? I doubt it. I think it's much more likely that He answered but we didn't listen. Maybe that's because we expected a *different kind of answer*.

Consider how David describes God's answer. David observes that he has been protected. Therefore, God answered. David does not limit the answer to a verbal reply, a spiritual feeling, the appearance of a prophet, the recollection of a favorite verse or a warm and fuzzy feeling of calm. David simply sees that his circumstances are altered. The invisible hand of God has interacted in the world of men. David has eyes to see what others never notice. God has answered.

For twenty-three days we have been searching in order to find peace. Perhaps it has been there all along but we have been so preoccupied with our own inner turmoil that we didn't notice. Perhaps we cried out but instead of seeing the answer from God according to *His* terms, we missed it entirely because we were looking for an answer in our terms. Now we need to notice *that God has already been at work*. The fact that we woke up today to reconsider once more our desires and our struggles is absolute proof that God has answered. Perhaps it's time to read this again.

http://skipmoen.com/2011/10/27/spiritual-grammar-2/

Today, Day 24, is the day that I remember that I am the continuous presence before YHVH, the continuous Father. Maybe "The Lord shepherds me" is another way to say "Day 23."

*Laurita writes;*

*What is existence? Psalm 103 tells me that the angels exist to obey His commandments, the hosts exist for His pleasure, and all exist to "bless the Lord". All obey that definition; all participate in their definition, may be a better statement, except the wicked hearts of men and fallen angels. The heavens declare the glory of G-d, and the earth shows His handiwork. We can look to all of His creation for a faithful transcript of His character; for knowledge of His identity; literally to see Who He Is, and we can trust that what we see is true, but "the heart of man is (desperately- continually- deceitfully) wicked". Why is it wicked? Because it does not, in fact, reflect accurately Who He Is. To be turned to His face is to be mirroring Himself back to Himself, which means that His glory is reflected back. This is how we bless Him: we show Him His handiwork, which is us! Conversely, I have learned that it is also to be able to see in Him who I am at the same time. We know this in a small way when we face each other, and do the same thing. I*

143

*know who I am when I see myself (literally) reflected in your eyes, and when I know you are listening, I can hear who I am through your ears. There is an aspect of my reality, in fact, that cannot exist without you. I do not even know who I am unless you are there to show (mirror it to) me.*

*Many cultures, I believe, have language that reflects this idea that a person in the singular does not exist, including the Hebrew culture in the Bible, where the smallest recognized unit is the family. You are recognized as who you are only in terms of who everyone is around you: you are known by your tribe, and your relationships: you are known by WHO YOU KNOW: who you admit into your circle. We do this even in our culture. We like to drop names and hang out with the winners, and brag about the accomplishments of our children(!) but I don't think we recognize it as being a valid definition of who we are in our identity, which is formally recognized only in the singular. This makes the behavior of Yeshua all that more radical, in that He seemed to make a point of hanging out with all the losers: He identified Himself with the poor in spirit, the mourners, the lowly, downtrodden and the forsaken. By associating Himself with them, He literally was making the statement that this was Who He Is. No one missed the point, and many "turned back from following Him." They didn't want to be associated with sinners and losers; that is not how they saw themselves. But G-d! He became us. I am overcome. He came to where I was, and faced me in my miserable lostness, and showed me who I was by showing me Who He Is. Now I don't know who I am unless I can know Who He Is. I have to start over in my identity, because Someone came to join my tribe. I have become a new person because He became who I am. He took on my identity for the purposes of giving me His. I am overcome. Overcome. What a word!*

*The answer to all my distress is already there, but He cannot give it to me unless and until I can face Him, for the answer is Himself. The day I am ready to face who I am, is the day I am going to have to face Who He Is, for, whether I liked it or not, He, by coming to me, and by facing me first, has changed my true identity. By dying in my place, He switched identities with me. To get who I am back, I now have to crawl up on that cross with Him so as to be transformed, through my death to Self, into His image, His identity. When I am covered by His blood, His Father sees Him when He looks at me. I can face Him when my sins are forgiven, and when I face Him, He can see Who He Is again. Hallelujah! Bless the Lord, O my soul!*

**25.** *I lay down and slept; I **awoke**, for the Lord sustains me.* Psalm 3:5 NASB

## Simple Things

Life as it is. Not life as I want it to be. Just what is now? That's where I find God. Just waking up. Oh, what a *joy*! God didn't decide my time was over when I went to bed last night. He has given me another day to fulfill *mitzvot*, enjoy His creation and change my life. I am alive! The world is good today.

We have been struggling with the emotions that accompany desiring life *as we wish it to be*. That is an endless exercise in *yetzer ha'ra* futility. Life will never be as we wish it to be because our wishing never ends. Remember that old joke, "How many millions does a millionaire need to be happy?" Answer: "Just one more." That's the path of the *yetzer ha'ra*. Just a little more. The life that is never satisfied with what is. The life that is always projected somewhere beyond today. No wonder we couldn't find peace. Peace is a present tense verb, not a wish in the future. Today is the day of salvation. If I am waiting for "heaven" (in whatever form I hope it to be) in order to find peace, I will never arrive. The kingdom of heaven is here. The *olam ha'ba* is *arriving*, not waiting for you to show up later. Moses Luzzatto's insight that we experience the presence of the divine and the favor of men as we fulfill the *mitzvot* here and in so doing cause the world to come to be manifest *here* is crucial for our happiness *here*. Few of us can postpone any form of human significance and emotional peace for a promise in the bye-and-bye.

"I awoke," writes David. One word in Hebrew. *Heqitsoti*. The verb is *yaqats*. Psalm 17:15 provides the comfort that waking up means experiencing His presence again. Then there is the great promise of Psalm 121:3-4: "He will not allow your foot to slip; He who keeps you will not slumber. Behold, He who keeps Israel will neither slumber nor sleep."

So we don't have to do it all on our own. We tire. We sleep exhausted from our struggles. We fall into unconscious non-existence. But YHVH does not. He is not a god who needs to be awakened. He is there even while we have collapsed. His mercies never fail us. His watchfulness does not evaporate. He is *'emet*—reliable, trustworthy, faithful. The gift God gave you today was being alive. The gratitude you show for that gift is found in your desire to honor Him. But desire is only motivation, not execution. The manifestation of that desire is seen in your willingness to adopt His ways as your ways. It is Ruth's expression of _hesed_. "Your people will be my people and your God will be my God." We all arrived as Ruth. Battered with suspicious backgrounds. Misfits and misunderstood. "Sometimes we wish the world could cry and tell us about that which made it pregnant with fear-filling grandeur. Sometimes we wish our own hearts would speak of that which made them heavy with wonder."[26] Awake! Awake to the overwhelming splendor of life—and breathe

---

[26] Abraham Heschel, *Man Is Not Alone*, p. 16.

in the spirit He gave so that you might revel in His wonder. Day 25.

*Laurita writes:*

*The angels sang at the birth of Messiah: "Peace on earth, good will toward men". When He came to tabernacle among us, He brought all the goodness of heaven with Him. Heaven emptied its entire treasure house, its most precious Gift, and sent Him to us. What gift was that? What did we need to be given? What did we lack? The angels announced the treasure. They were the label on our Package. The shepherds opened it for us. The Gift was amnesty; the Gift announced that we can quit the war now. We don't have to fall for the lies any more, for the Truth just showed up to show us what we were missing, and that is the truth that we are loved. We forgot that, and when we forgot, we fell for the lies about love. Then Love came.*

*Love came to unpack the Law for us. He came to show us a picture of what that Law was supposed to look like: a picture of Love with flesh on, a picture of perfect homeostasis with both heaven, earth, and the entire cosmos in between. Love is about peace, harmony; and when the angels sing, they put that harmony into their song, and the air becomes liquid with that love. The angels gave us the best fingernail synopsis of the Law ever given. It is an even better one than the one the lawyer quoted for Yeshua from Deuteronomy, for it gives us what obedience to the first Four and the last Six Commands looks like in execution. The angels' song was no command: it was completion. He came to restore that completion, that perfection, to us; came*

148

*to give us in His own Body that peace that the rest of the universe and heaven enjoys with its Maker, as well as peace among our war-torn selves. We defied heaven itself, and operated from a complete lack of trust of each other; we broke the Law in so many ways, and this was heaven's response. We really don't know what Love is. We lost all the clues in the dark: we lost the light switch too, and then we fell for the lie that we needed it to be dark, so we didn't even go look. So the Light of men came to us.*

*I am lost in wonder.*

*The Law is about the steps for fallen man to take to restore his broken relationship with G-d, himself, and everyone else. The Law, in other words, is about peace. I think the worst lie we ever fell for was the one that told us we did not need the Law to have peace. Peace is the state of obedience to that Law! If you were caught for speeding, and endangering the lives of others and yourself on the road, and came before the judge, should he then say "I can see this is a bad law, because it got broken: I am going to fix your disobedience by annulling the law about speeding"? Yet, when it comes to G-d's Law, we can, and do, say nonsense such as this with a straight face, and after long deliberation; even by people with enough degrees of education, so-called, to make a pot of alphabet soup with. Sigh. This has to be the single most breathtaking, audacious presumption of grace that we could have ever devised! And then we accuse Yeshua of coming to annul His own Law of Peace! Worse and worse! May heaven forgive us! Someone please turn on the light!*

*The very air we breathe, and the breath in our nostrils, is about an advance; a down payment of harmony with the Breath-Giver and with reality, and life itself, that we are not, in fact, yet in agreement with. It is sheer grace that enables me to wake up in the morning, but I presume on that grace when I take it for granted, and forget to turn around and reciprocate with humility and gratitude for that measure of time that grace affords me. Gratitude restores the opportunity for a right relationship with the Giver, but I remain ungrateful to the extent that I am presuming on that grace by neglecting to take advantage of that opportunity. It is a dangerous lie we are skating on when we believe that grace actually restores peace to us. Just because I am still alive does not necessarily mean that I am getting it right; nor does it follow that Someone else got it right for me! Grace is not, in fact, a restoration of peace: grace is not fulfillment of the Law that is the picture of that peace. Therefore, just because I am still breathing does not mean that that breath is actually doing me any good. There is still my part. That air also means that my ears can hear, and that my eyes can see. "Today, if you will hear his voice, harden not your hearts". Gratitude for His grace and mercy keeps my heart amenable to His voice.*

**26.** *For there are many words which increase futility. What then is the advantage to a man?* Ecclesiastes 6:11 NASB

## *Information*

We are the most informed generation of human beings to ever walk the planet. We know quite a bit about quite a bit. But we know almost nothing about what really matters. Believing that we will find the soul-peace we so desperately desire by accumulating more information (about God, the Bible, the Church, ourselves or anything else) is a ploy of the *yetzer ha'ra*, convincing us that we can control and predict; we can exercise power over even the foibles of the *yetzer ha'ra*. It is a shell game. You lose!

"As civilization advances, the sense of wonder almost necessarily declines. Such decline is an alarming symptom of our state of mind. Mankind will not perish for want of information; but only for want of appreciation. The beginning of our happiness lies in the understanding that life without wonder is not worth living. What we lack is not a will to believe but a will to wonder."[27]

Today I walked (rather than drive) three miles along a busy road. As I walked, I noticed what God did— and what we have done. In the ditch, next to discarded soda cans and plastic bags, were tiny

---

[27] Abraham Heschel, *Man Is Not Alone*, p. 37.

purple flowers, each one an exquisite masterpiece in design and function. Beautifully enhanced with graduated shades of nature's kaleidoscope, one could only be in awe that God would take such care of these lilies of the field while we throw our substitutes of functional expediency on top of His carpet of splendor.

We use religious words in the same way we use Styrofoam. Convenient, cheap containers for transporting ideas from one mind to another. "There would, indeed, be no greater comfort than to live in the security of foregone conclusions, if not for that gnawing concern which turns all conclusions into a shambles."[28]

Heschel has articulated our need and the steps we must take to avoid the temptation of simply mouthing solutions.

"Faith is not a product of our will. It occurs without intention, without will. Words expire when uttered, and faith is like the silence that draws lovers near, like a breath that shares the wind."[29] We are "a parenthesis in the immense script of God's eternal speech,"[30] and because it is God who is speaking, all of our verbal pretentions are interruptions to the majesty of His voice. There is only one response appropriate for us. Praise. "Unless we know how to praise Him, we cannot learn how to know Him."[31] What we need desperately, the sense of belonging to the great symphony of God, can only

---

[28] Ibid., p. 71.
[29] Ibid., p. 73.
[30] Ibid., p. 75
[31] Ibid., p. 74.

be experienced in a state of awe. Today, Day 25, is "wonder day." Hear with your eyes the harmonies of the spheres. Find that tiny purple flower that opens your way into the eternal. Praise Him, praise Him, praise Him. Today He allows you to utter speechless exclamations of joy. Today you are a part of the cosmic choir.

*Laurita writes:*

*"Without faith it is impossible to please him" for, whatsoever is not of faith is sin". But, here is the rub: I cannot generate even the first iota of faith! Without it I cannot even step out of sin into obedience; in fact, all my obedience is counted as filthy rags – as symbols of unfruitfulness and futility – without the faith that righteousness must have to operate in. Without faith, I cannot even see my sin, for that requires that I have faith that what the Law is showing me is true, but it also takes faith to repent, because I cannot turn around if I did not have faith in another Way. It takes faith to walk in that Way, too, because when I am not traveling on my own orders and following what I think must be so, I am having to exercise faith that Someone Else's orders and will are best for me. That takes a lot of faith! Further, all the fruits of the Spirit can only occur in the presence of faith; faith is the only context in which they can bear fruit. "Love, joy, peace, longsuffering, gentleness, goodness, faith, meekness, temperance": oh, how hard I tried to employ every one, but to no avail, in my flesh! I learned the hard way that they are fruits, or, results, or even aftereffects, if you will, of the presence of the Holy Spirit in my life. If He is not free to employ*

154

*each one in season, for His purposes, and in His Way (not mine!), they, in turn, will not bear the "peaceable fruit of righteousness" in my life – none of them will do me, or anybody else, any good! I, then, have to have faith that the Holy Spirit will generate His fruit in my life, before I am going to quit trying to do that on my own. I am going to have to trust Him to reproduce His righteousness in me before I can hand over the reins of my attempts to obey.*

*I think some people can get confused about what faith is; they can think that faith is a mental assent to a set of doctrines, or even that faith is what we must 'do' to obtain salvation ("have faith in Jesus!") However, the Bible shows me that faith, properly understood, is about trust – but trust is exactly what I lack! Trust, in fact, is what breaks when I sin, or even when others sin against me; all sin destroys trust, but trust is what I am told I must have to obey! The first order of business, then, is to replace the trust it takes to do right. Now, just how do I do that?*

*To restore my function in creation, which is to enjoy all that I have been given (for my pleasure is His, as any lover will testify, and I was literally created for His pleasure – Rev. 4:11), I have to be able to walk in each instant with full wonder: I must take each breath, and think each thought – make each decision – and initiate each action in the blindness to Self that the "substance of things hoped for; the evidence of things not yet seen" must have to operate in. My pleasure is the reason of that entire creation, and my pleasure, then, is how I reflect that creation back properly to Him. Each instant of*

155

*unmitigated wonder is true service – is true worship of my Creator, for that pleasure honors why that creation exists. However, I must be free before I can enjoy it. This is the freedom that only trust can know, but it is a freedom that bondage to Self can never know. Therefore, I must ignore the service of Self to serve Him, but that entails that I "walk by faith, and not by sight". If I do not have the freedom of choices that faith returns to me, however, I also do not have the simultaneous freedom of the pleasure that that choice entails, for pleasure is only possible when I perceive that there is no other reason – no mitigating factors for it other than that I happen to like what is in front of me. I cannot enjoy something that I suspect does not have my best interests at heart. I find that I do not wonder at the universe because I do not, in fact, trust it!*

*A child learns early to be suspicious of pleasure that ensnares with covert motives. How often do we bribe our infants with the distracting toy, when we perhaps should have respected his or her unhappiness as a symptom of a need – and then we wonder why that child grew up unable to recognize his or her needs, but instead employs the distraction of loaded pleasure – pleasure that comes packaged with a covert reason to exist! "Simple pleasures", it seems, are pleasures that we have not corrupted with the sin of distraction from our true condition. This is simply impossible to find in the flesh, for the flesh always has an ulterior motive! And why is that? Because the flesh just doesn't trust anyone or anything! Pleasure then, in the original sense of creation, is impossible to attain in the flesh, because it appears that even pleasure for its own sake requires faith!*

156

*So how do I get that mythical golden ball back? How do I get back to the place of full and unreserved trust? I want my mojo back! To walk in wonder is to walk in trust. "Except ye be converted, and become as little children, ye shall not enter into the kingdom of heaven." I have to get back to the vulnerability of childhood: back to that place where my identity was inseparable from that of my parents; back to that aching place where my every moment was couched in the pleasure (or displeasure) of my parents. I have to be born again to another Father; this time, however, to One that I can fully trust! Hallelujah! This is where the real fun starts! In the service of the kingdom of Self, the only dubious pleasure is me(!), but when I am born again into the kingdom of my heavenly Father, I get the entire universe as my playpen: every pleasure in it is mine, and He "withholds no good thing" from me.*

**27.** *You will make known to me the path of life; in Your presence is fullness of joy; in Your right hand there are pleasures forever.* Psalm 16:11 NASB

## Three Dog Night

We are often taught that joy cannot be manufactured, that it is a passionate, subjective experience that overcomes us. At the same time, we learn that joy is not dependent on our circumstances. Unlike happiness, joy is a product of involvement in the presence of the Lord or the wealth of community, even community with the created world. Perhaps joy is really the byproduct of deep reflection, of the realization that my very being in the world is best understood as an essential measure in the great symphony. Perhaps joy is knowing that who I am and what I do matters. "We become alive to our living in the great fellowship of all beings, we cease to regard things as opportunities to exploit."[32]

Joy is the speechless response to the question, "How shall we ever reciprocate for breathing and thinking, for sight and hearing, for love and achievement?"[33] *I am joy. You are joy.* Just being in the palm of His creating is enough to bring joy for He only does what has purpose and meaning. As Heschel remarks, you and I are a "transcendent loan" to the world; a statement of YHVH's trust in His choice to create agents like Himself. Joy is realizing that He cares about me.

---

[32] Abraham Heschel, *Man Is Not Alone*, p. 39.
[33] Ibid.

158

This is why a man or woman without a sense of greater purpose is empty of joy. Yes, such person can certainly find happiness but happiness is fleeting and requires a constant adjustment of circumstances in order to satisfy. Happiness rides on the rails of "one more." Joy is a different-order experience. It is the experience of overwhelming purpose, of knowing somehow that I count in the great scheme of things. Joy is an encounter with beyond myself, a face-to-face with the reality of the infinitesimal and the infinite. Joy is not a thing or a collection of things nor can it be produced by my engagement with things. Joy is the space between words that gives the meaning of the sentence. When I look for it, it cannot be found because it exists only in the in-between of my actions, and only in the in-between of my actions that extend beyond me, that involve the purposes of the Creator. Joy is *nephesh hayyah* before *'ayyekkah*.*

Some days ago we started with the quest for peace. Now we have discovered that well-being is not our real goal. Well-being is the state of bliss that accompanies joy and joy is the by-product of exercising created and creative purpose. We want *shalom* because we know all too well its absence, but *shalom* is the rainbow of heaven, something seen but impossible to grasp. This rainbow *occurs* when the arrangement of light and water is at the proper angle to the observer. *Shalom* is not something I generate. It is there, always, in the proper angle, the angle of relationship between the breath of our Creator and our position in the creation. God breathes—and if I am found in the right place at the right time I will experience the joy

159

of His breath as me making a difference in the world.

Did you notice that David claims that God is the causal agent in this relation? He will make known. In His presence I will find. His right hand is full. It's not me. He acts. I receive. But in order to receive I must be where I am supposed to be—in the place where heaven's rainbow witnesses to His promise. Day 27.

*nephesh hayyah* before *'ayyekkah*. If God has to ask, "Where are you?" then you aren't in the right place.

\* "living person" before "Where are you?"

*Laurita writes:*

*"The joy of the Lord is my strength." "A three-fold cord is not easily broken." We have had it pointed out to us that we are only as strong as our weakest link. When I make a move to fulfill my purpose, which I also believe is that "essential measure in the great symphony" (I love all the quotes!) I am making a move to participate in providing strength to all else. How do I do that? Is this going to sound trite? I do it by holding hands; by aligning myself with the interests of others without qualification, for I need all, and am needed by all. My strength is your strength. His joy comes from His children harmonizing, and that harmony is what makes us strong. When I please my Father, His joy then fills my tank, and I no longer need the crutches of addictive sin or the blinders of altered states of*

*reality to get through my day. Doing right then means I no longer have to do wrong.*

*Joy comes from the absence of chaos, then. It comes from the areas of my life that have been restored to the function of purpose. Those areas are my 'strong points'. In those places, the pleasure of my Father overtakes me and I ride the wind.*

**28.** *and after he brought them out, he said, "Sirs, what must I do to be **saved**?"* Acts 16:30 NASB

## Where Are You?

"Religions may be classified as those of self-satisfaction, of self-annihilation or of fellowship. In the first worship is a quest for satisfaction of personal needs like salvation or desire for immortality. In the second all personal needs are discarded, and man seeks to dedicate his life to God at the price of annihilating all desire, believing that human sacrifice or at least complete self-denial is the only true form of worship. The third form of religion, while shunning the idea of considering God a means for attaining personal ends, insists that there is a partnership of God and man, that human needs are God's concern, and that divine ends ought to become human needs. It rejects the idea that the good should be done in self-detachment, that the satisfaction felt in doing good would taint the purity of the act."[34]

Heschel continues: "The sense of moral obligation remains impotent unless it is stronger than all other obligations, stronger than the stubborn power of self- interests. To compete with selfish inclinations the moral obligation must be allied with the highest passion of the spirit. To be stronger than evil, the moral imperative must be more powerful than the passion for evil. An abstract norm, an ethereal idea, is no match for the gravitation of the ego. Passion can only be subdued by stronger passion."[35]

---

[34] Abraham Heschel, *Man Is Not Alone*, p. 250.
[35] Ibid., p. 251.

If we are going to find deliverance from the clutches of the *yetzer ha'ra*, we must find a *passion for God*. Since the *yetzer ha'ra* already commands our sense of self-entitlement and controls our desire for self-fulfillment, we cannot turn to those avenues for help. They have already been co-opted by the enemy within. We will have to enlist a force stronger than our craving for pleasure and self-protection. We will have to enlist the force YHVH has already supplied in hidden abundance—awe. Awe in the face of the abundance of life itself. Awe over the enormity of existence. Awe that shatters our pretentions to power, our penchant for personal importance. We will have to run to the fields and stare into the heaven on a moonless night. We will have to contemplate the construction of a lily, the flight of a butterfly, the shocking reality of a lightning bolt. We will have to *taste* the rain, *breathe* the scent of lilacs, *feel* the skin of a newborn, *hear* the roar of a lion in order to appreciate the wonder of living for it is the wonder of living that overpowers our self-centered *yetzer ha'ra*. No man can sin in the midst of awe. Humility, gratitude, exhilaration, fellowship come from awe-full saturation. The revolt of the *yetzer ha'ra* attempts to numb us to the reality of the magnificent.

You and I are religious people. But which religion is ours? Have we worshipped in order to fill some need? Are we "saved" because we have obtained something from our God? Did we practice the rituals because we wished to deny the complexity of our human reality, because we wanted to rid ourselves of the thorny branches of choice? Unless we enter into fellowship, into the searing convolutions of struggle with partnership, the *idea of God* will never deliver us from the passions that direct our lives. Salvation is discovered, not obtained, by participating in the wonder of His purposes. We will have to enlist in the cosmic conflict if the power of the Spirit is going to resurrect us.

*Laurita writes:*

*"We will have to enlist in the cosmic conflict if the power of the Spirit is going to resurrect us."*
*What is the purpose that is bigger than me? It is the purpose of my Creator. What is He engaged in? Is He indifferent to the evil in His realm, or did He not send His Man into the thick of the fray? And if He is engaged, then does He not call me to enlist in His service, and can I not then expect to stand shoulder to shoulder with Him in the recovery of His kingdom on this earth? If I am going to relate to Him, then His interests must become mine.*

*I read the account of the conflict on Mount Carmel this morning; the conflict between Baal worship and the worship of YHVH. The people wanted it both ways. They wanted the benefits of both; they wanted to mingle the divine with the profane. Elijah wanted to bring this terrible cause of the drought to its head. He wanted a contest between the two, so that they would no longer be confused. So, he devised a test of power. It was a test that moved the worship of both into the supernatural realm. The top of Carmel was neutral ground in that neither worship had a source there: neither worship had an*

164

*altar fire already burning. The altar fire was going*
*to have to be kindled anew. We know the story.*
*After trying all day, by efforts both in faith (praying*
*and self-mutilation) and in secret (they surely tried*
*to light that fire in secret themselves, which Elijah*
*had to watch out for), they gave up.*

*The fire from heaven was a fire that consumed both*
*the sacrifice and the altar, along with the water*
*(anti-fire). The fire from heaven is a fire that*
*baptizes with the intent to consume all of the*
*profane in my life. It will overcome the feeble efforts*
*I make in self-defense against it, it will burn the*
*fleshly altar I build to offer my sacrifice on, too. In*
*fact, I am promised that if I bring the sacrifice that*
*is pleasing to Him, which is the "Sacrifices of God*
*is a broken spirit; A broken and a contrite heart, O*
*God, You will not despise." Psalms 51:17, He*
*promises to burn all the dross and leave only the*
*pure. Only that which cannot be corrupted is*
*pleasing to Him. When His image is perfected in me,*
*He is satisfied. Can I build such an image? No. Can*
*I offer the best of my efforts, like Cain? No. Can I*
*sacrifice what I please: can I INVENT the worship I*
*wish to worship Him with? No. What does He want*
*me to bring? He does not even want me to show up*
*until I can come with that "broken spirit"! Why?*
*Because my spirit must be replaced with His. Only*
*contrition and repentance create the condition in*
*which my heart can be safely transferred out, and*
*His be transplanted in, for it is only in the turning*
*away from sin that I am safely separated from my*
*interests and alliances with that sin. Why is this*
*necessary? Because when I am delivered from my*
*disobedience and freed from the curse of that sin*
*into the opportunity to obey, my sin gets destroyed,*

*but He will not make a move to hurt me, so He waits until I turn loose; until I turn around. David prayed that the Spirit of YHVH be not taken from him, when he sinned. He brought his broken and contrite spirit to that request. He turned around. He knew the sacrifice that pleased the Lord.*

*The yetzer ha-ra knows nothing of awe, for awe is humility in the face of that which is bigger than I, but the yetzer ha-ra will admit nothing into its kingdom bigger than itself. The desires of my flesh consume me on the altar I build to worship myself. Both religions, if you will, demand the sacrifice of ME. Both will consume me: both are going to kill me, but only one can give me a new birth. "That which is born of the flesh is flesh, and that which is born of the Spirit is spirit." John 3:6. When my fleshly heart, which is hard as a rock because it is completely inhuman(!) gets traded for a heart that is built out of flesh (I am returned to who I really am, like Ezekiel 36:26 promises), that verse also promises that I will be given a new spirit in my nephesh: I will be re-powered with the baptism of fire from heaven, and Pentecost will be my continual reality. This is the heart that is big enough to comprehend His purposes, and is connected to the Source of the love necessary to carry them out. Further, because I will have that Spirit of complete submission, which is His, for my own, the awe that comes as the side effect of true submission will be the awe that fills my days and is the worship that is acceptable to Him. I will be reflecting Himself back to Himself, then, which is my acceptable service. Hallelujah!*

166

**29.** *If I have the gift of prophecy, and know all mysteries and **all knowledge**; and if I have all faith, so as to remove mountains, but do not have love, I am nothing.* 1 Corinthians 13:2 NASB

## *What Difference Does It Make?*

Day 28. We are coming close. But lest we imagine that these last days are about gaining knowledge in order to get a grip on the elusive "spiritual" life, we need to consider Paul's declaration (lament?). "If I understand all knowledge." The Greek text is *eido pantan gnosin,* implying not merely sensory perception but a deep penetration into the essence of things. In other words, the same kind of knowledge that God Himself has. Paul uses the strongest possible case, what we would call *omniscience.* Even if I know everything that can be known but I am without love, I am *nothing!* This is powerful. Even a "god" without love (and we have yet to determine what "love" is) is nothing!

So here we are. Rational, discursive, analytic, predictive, cognitive, controlling beings gathering information in order to govern our unruly emotional lives. And Paul says, "Collect as much as you can. Stuff yourselves with knowing. Then recognize that it means *nothing at all* unless it is employed in the service of love." Twenty-eight days into analysis we come to the brick wall of arrogance. We thought we could figure all of this out. We thought we could somehow lasso our emotions and get them under control. We thought we were capable of redirecting the *yetzer ha'ra,* that slippery and conning force, through the strength of our understanding. We thought we could *save ourselves* (with a little help from on high, of course). But Paul sets us straight. All mysteries, all knowledge, all prophecy—none of it makes any difference, not even to YHVH Himself, unless we encounter love. And that cannot be accomplished at all—unless the love of YHVH first encounters us.

In the end it isn't intellectual prowess that leads me out of the pit. In fact, intellectual prowess is more than likely my enemy. It convinces me that what I lack is the magic formula of spiritual awareness when the truth is that what I lack is the fear of the Lord. In the end I must come to terms with my *created* status, my utter dependence on mercy and grace, my emptiness, the depths that I fear to see. In the end, knowing brings me to nothing.

The whisper. That's what I need. The whisper that makes it all make sense. The whisper that tells me I am His concern. No more analysis. No more word studies of amazing insights. No more explanations and explications. No, now I must listen for the whisper. I must compel the ear of the universe to hear the faintest praise of the Creator in order to know that He sees something in my blind eyes. What is this love that Paul prioritizes? It is *agape*, the spontaneous passive experience of being cared for, of being someone's concern. It is not knowing that a declaration of care is true. It is *feeling* it as a visceral reality in my life. I need the whisper of the lover of my soul in order to be whole. Nothing less will do.

If you are interested in the exegetical analysis of the "love" chapter of 1 Corinthians, you might read this. http://skipmoen.com/2008/03/05/the-grammar-of-love/


*Laurita writes:*

*Michael Stanley, I miss you in all the places you have not written something! You just sliced sideways into the tumor of my previous life. And made me laugh, and remember, when you did. Thank you!*

*I have hesitated to respond to this day's discourse, because it lays open the deepest wound of my life. In fact, the rest of my little tragedies perhaps were self-imposed flights into the unknown wilderness that I chose to participate in in an unknowing attempt to avoid that deepest cut, which is the call of the Damascus Road that I think comes to everyone in some form or another.*

*"For the gifts and calling of God are without repentance" Romans 11:29. I was born with the instinct to hide my deepest self from myself, as well as all others, including G-d. I can never remember a time when I did not ache with the pain of that shame. The pretense of pride goes all the way back. At no time did I truly believe that it would be ok if I revealed who I truly was. At no time did I not suffer viscerally from not being able to. Hiding is excruciating!*

*As I hit my teen years, I held out a hope that it was at least external circumstances that prevented me*

170

*from being able to walk freely in the land of the living in my own skin, strong and unafraid. I longed to reveal who I really was, and to operate from that platform. By then, I was starting to sense the difficulty that exposure entailed, and that it was going to cost something. I was hurting badly enough by then to start to be willing to endure the pain of disclosure as an alternative; I still believed, wanted to believe, in my relative innocence, anyway – I wanted to believe that it was only because I had not gotten a "real chance" to "express myself"!*

*So I embarked on a journey of self-discovery, aching from the pain of shame the whole way, and I actually managed to get quite a ways along; far enough to decide that I needed a medium of expression; a way to communicate to others who I 'really was'. I would go to that hurting place where I could hear the throbbing of all my sorrow and all my desire for joy, and lay my hand on that wall that was constructed to keep who I was from myself, and then try. I systematically attempted to pick up the mediums that I saw (and appreciated) others using. I tried all the art forms I could get my hands on the tools for, as I saw art as a way I wanted to 'see myself' through – in each one, one by one, I would get to a point of proficiency, whether it was visual arts; drawing and painting, or music, or even poetry, and then, I would hit a wall. It wasn't that I particularly lacked any skill, it was that I didn't have ENOUGH skill to unlock the door in that wall of me. I got more and more upset.*

*It was finally, in response to an insightful teacher who assigned an open-ended writing essay, that I stumbled upon that elusive flash: I had actually*

171

*found a wave to ride, and I happily rode it, hurting all the way, sure that what I had to say was so offensive it would not even get graded; but, it got a favorable response – actual encouragement – on the other end! I was ecstatic. However, just as quickly, my joy turned to, well, incredulous rage. I couldn't believe it. The modicum of expression I had the single biggest love-hate relationship with, which was the words of prose, no less, was the only thing I had found a voice in. I protested. I didn't WANT words! By that time, I didn't trust words any more. In fact, I had the deepest suspicion that words CONCEALED truth; that words only showed up in the place Thoreau described as a "lull in the wind": and prose, no less! Not even the mystical, magical rivers of Syria, but the muddy, floody Jordan – that river that connected the Land of Promise to the wilderness of my disasters, which I was seeking asylum from! I got very angry. I protested: I denied: I pouted. I despised words and all they represented, because they had let me down the most. So I turned my back, and when life intervened in my education, I was glad to run from the pain that the path of self-disclosure represented. I didn't write again for over 20 years.*

*Here I am again. I still believe that words can conceal the truth; that we depend on them in fact, in so many ways, to do just that. I think we turn to knowledge that words represent as a weapon against ourselves; as insulation from the truth – the truth of who we really are. In fact, my suspicion has deepened into conviction that the truth, the real Truth, is wordless. As such, words, and their underlying knowledge, are my bane, in the fullest sense of the word. They represent blessing, and*

172

*curse, and destiny for me. I sweat every time I have to use them, fully aware that if I were to truly use them effectively, I would need none of them. I am sweating now.*

*I have a son of few words. We can be together, traveling or working or just hanging out, and hours can pass, where we interact with each other, just hanging out on each other's wave length, and no words are necessary. In that place, the truth shows up. When I was young, I heard a song about a boy who struck a note "that sounded like a great Amen", and he spent the rest of his life searching for it again. I think love resonates fully only in the place beyond all knowledge, and we ache until we rest in Him.*

**30.** *Therefore, to one who knows the right thing to do and does not do it, to him it is **sin**.* James 4:17 NASB

## Sin with Purpose

We are familiar with the exhortation that awareness of our sin is one of the purposes of Torah. In this sense, Torah is the schoolteacher, showing us where and when we have gone astray so that we might plead for merciful return to His presence. In this context, we often find theologians characterizing sin as something "insane" (e.g., Berkouwer). After all, what rational man would deliberately choose a pathway that absolutely puts his entire life in danger and guarantees horrendous punishment? The insanity of sin makes sense. But maybe there is another aspect of our disobedience that needs to be illuminated in order for us to recognize the signs before the fall.

What happens to us when we sin? (By the way, notice that James assumes a certain common understanding of disobedience along with individual application). First we must take notice of the fact that very rarely do we experience the immediate consequences of our actions. This delay allows the *yetzer ha'ra* to operate, suggesting either that God doesn't really care or that God will certainly forgive at a later time (when *we* require it). When we do experience the inevitable guilt, remorse and moral confusion, we are inclined to immediately appropriate grace in any attempt to circumvent any future repetition of our mistake. And we usually fail. The reason we fail is not that we didn't understand the requirement; rather, it is that we did not pay attention to the sign along the way. We did not consider (or we deliberately ignored) those lesser acts that brought us to the point of sinful behavior, a point where we are without willpower to prevent the consequent disobedience. Sin is orgasmic. There is a point of no return. There is a point where, no matter what you wish to do, it's simply too late to stop. The key to righteous behavior is to divert the causal connections *before* they reach the explosive edge. And here sin itself becomes purposeful.

We sin. But instead of running to the altar, perhaps we should consider for a moment what sequence of events and actions preceded our sin. We find one link in the causal chain that we know will lead us into disobedience. We correct that *one* link. For example, if I find that each time I am with certain friends at a ball game I exaggerate the truth (i.e., I lie) in order to impress them, then I correct that situation by insuring that I do not attend a game with these people. Step one. On further observation (and more sin), I realize that it is not just the friends and the circumstances that cause this behavior. I notice that it occurs only after I have had a disagreement with my spouse. Another correction is necessary further up the causal chain. I sin again. Now I have to step even further back, recognizing that the reason for the argument with my spouse finds its source in my going to work without taking time to pray in the morning. Another backward step. As you can see, ultimately the goal is to identify those basic steps that lead me to sinful actions so that I can avoid the steps *before* I get to the unstoppable end. Perhaps instead of fighting to exhaustion those unstoppable ends I would be better served by examining what happened before I was no longer able to control the outcome. Each time I do this, I back up until at last I see the path before it becomes a choice—and I choose another way. I use the power of the *yetzer ha'ra* against itself.

If we are going to really make any progress toward righteousness we will have to find ways to short-circuit those patterns we have conditioned ourselves to use as ways of numbing our fears. With the help of YHVH, perhaps this is seeking Him too.

*Laurita writes:*

*"I use the power of the yetzer ha-ra against itself." Ho, ho; now we come to the meat of the matter.*

*"Therefore if thou bring thy gift to the altar, and there remember that thy brother hath ought against thee, leave there thy gift before the altar, and go thy way; first be reconciled to thy brother (Torah obedience) and then come offer thy gift." Matt. 5:23,24. YHVH apparently doesn't even want to have anything to do with us until we have something to do with each other! Hmm.*

*A friend reminded me yesterday about a prayer group that had invited me to come share my experience in recovering from all the illness and debility in my life, which was my testimony. I had agreed, and had started out walking them through the steps that I had taken to get to my freedom. Well, we made it through the understanding that healing is for today, and that it is a consequence of the restoration of relationships. We talked about accusation and how to recognize it and how it opens the door to the rest of it. We made it through a discussion on bitterness, which is the chronic state of unforgiveness, and got all the way to the point in the Lord's Prayer where it talks about forgiving others as a precondition to us being forgiven by G-d, and the whole thing came apart. I mean, the whole room rose up. When I asked what the problem was, almost all of them, to a man (well, it was a men's group, after all!) protested that they felt that their salvation was being challenged; and they all went into fear. No matter how I approached it, they could not deal with it. If their salvation was going to be conditional upon their ability to forgive, then they didn't want to hear it. I didn't get invited back.*

*When Skip talks about backing up that path of the wrong choices, which is the wrong reactions to the challenges and unknowns of my life, until I get to the original fork, he is describing exactly what I have had to learn to do. I am not going to be delivered of fear, say, unless and until I am willing to face, and re-choose, every wrong belief, and every reaction based on those successive beliefs, until I make it back to the bottom fracture of trust that sent me into that fear. After all, I am afraid in all the places I do not trust.*

*I can cast out a spirit of fear all day long; I can claim salvation all the day long; I can blame the devil and invoke the blood until the going down of the sun, but until I become willing to face – and lament – the fact that I am the one who is angry because trust got broken and betrayed, and that the only right thing to do with that anger is to choose to hesed and to hen; to literally extend a fresh chance to that relationship: in fact, until I choose to act like my Saviour acted toward me, and come to the altar hand-in-hand with my brother, like He did with me, in His eyes, I don't even exist.*

*Existence, I have become convinced, must be a collective term. We need each other to even do the stuff. If I cannot allow you to exist – which bitterness does not allow, for it is murder in my heart – then I have, in effect, bound myself with cursed chains to the corpse I killed, which is a death sentence for me, too. In the ancient world, where this was a common form of torture, no one lasted over a few days. Bitterness is a killer. We destroy each other with our unforgiveness, but at the same time, we destroy ourselves. No salvation can come in between such a self-imposed sentence.*

# AND ONE MORE

*You will seek Me and find Me when you **search** for Me with all your heart.* Jeremiah 29:13 NASB

## *End Game*

Thirty days of self-examination. Thirty days of drawing closer, of recognizing the grace of the Father, the mystery of His care and concern, the depths of our need. Thirty days to begin something new again.

Perhaps we have examined this verse many times (see http://skipmoen.com/?s=Jeremiah+29%3A13). You might think there isn't much more to say but Isaiah disagrees. In Isaiah 11:10, we who were once far off (namely, Gentiles) will be the ones who will seek the Messiah as King of all God's children. With Isaiah's context we learn that every act of seeking the Kingdom is eschatological, that is to say, every time we fulfill a commandment or act with righteous intent, we are at the same time announcing the coming reign of the Messiah and the return of God's rule to the earth. On this last day of our brief journey we discover one more reason, one further motivation for pressing to the limit with the help of the Spirit. It isn't only that we matter to God. What we do matters to the restoration of God's reign. God has given over to us the final chapter in the return to well-being. We seek Him in order to find who we are and why we matter. He seeks us in order to bring about the restoration. The reason we pursue Him is because He pursues us. The end game is a double-edged search. It is the universe and the Creator in search of an answer. The only question left to you and me is this: Will you join Him?

Will we journey together? We will allow Him to find us? Will we become comrades in the quest?

It is quite impossible to say now how this journey will go and who will come along. In the end, that really doesn't seem to matter too much. Today I can experience the surprise of discovering that God is seeking me, and that I am searching with great care for Him. Today I can be doubly aware of those patterns that divert me from His fellowship on the way. Today I can act with selfless abandonment. Today is the day I can reset the clock, experience the wonder of living and find love in my heart for His grace.

God is calling. "Whom shall we send?"

### Hinneni

*Laurita writes:*

*The search for the answer is the Way from "Me" to the restoration of "We". As salvation cannot be accomplished without the joint cooperation of the saved and the Savior, the restoration of the Kingdom cannot be accomplished without the joint cooperation of the saved with each other and with heaven. We have been suffering a massive power outage from a cosmic storm, and we can only get it all turned back on when we have perfected the connections between the fractures. The kingdom of*

*"I" assumes that power originates with me; the Kingdom of Heaven assures us that the Power station that generates the love we all need is a function of the space in between.*

*As the gospel is so simple that even a child can grasp it, I think our main theological confusions must all arise from long centuries of pagan influence. The church of Self has corrupted our understanding of the beginning – the Source – as well as the application. Starting from Self, as paganism does, we appropriate the language of heaven to serve in our temples, and mass confusion has resulted. We assume that G-d wants to be like us, so we ascribe to Him our desired characteristics – which is pagan to the core – and we then accuse Him of motives so awful, and of a character so sinister, no wonder we run in fear.*

*Salvation is where G-d seeks us. It is His move toward us. Repentance, then, which is simply turning around in the Hebrew understanding, is how we seek Him back. I can rest assured that my rebellion has all consisted of running away (LOL!), so I can also rest assured that seeking Him with all my heart is going to consist of halting that flight, and turning around. He never left me: I turned my back.*

*The answers we are all seeking are not in the realm of knowledge, so words are not going to give them to us. The answer to our problem is to find a Power switch, and get our lights back on. The dark is a function of the fracture of connection, so I am going to be able to see if and only when I reach out and touch somebody else. The answer to my need is going to be found when I reach out to meet you in yours, for we share the same problem: we need each other. This has nothing to do with secret mysteries or mystical enlightenment; this has everything to do with the fact that I lost myself when I lost you.*

*Did you find this little book helpful?*

*Why not give a copy to someone you know?*

You can purchase this book, and support the work, by ordering from

skipmoen.com/products

Thank you.